Home Int.

$5

ORIENTAL RUGS

ALSO BY
JANICE SUMMERS HERBERT

Affordable Oriental Rugs: The Buyer's Guide to Rugs from China, India, Pakistan, and Romania

ORIENTAL RUGS

The Illustrated Guide

REVISED AND EXPANDED EDITION

BY

JANICE SUMMERS HERBERT

MACMILLAN PUBLISHING CO., INC.

NEW YORK

COLLIER MACMILLAN PUBLISHERS

LONDON

Photo Credits:
Jacques Bodenmann: Plates 46, 90, 91, 92, 94, 95, 96, 97, 98, 99, 100; *Bill Collins:* Plates
60, 89; *Theodore Herbert:* Plates 1, 3, 4, 5; *Richard LeNoir:* 2, 6, 7, 8, 9, 10, 11, 12, 13,
14, 15, 16, 17, 18, 19, 20, 21, 22, 23, 24, 25, 26, 27, 28, 29, 30, 31, 32, 33, 34, 35, 36, 37,
38, 39, 40, 41, 42, 43, 44, 45, 47, 48, 49, 50, 51, 52, 53, 54, 55, 56, 57, 58, 59, 61, 62, 63, 64,
66, 67, 69, 70, 71, 72, 73, 75, 76, 77, 78, 79, 80, 81, 82, 84, 85, 86, 87, 93, 102, 103, 104, 105,
106, 107, 108, 110, 111, 112, 113, 114, 115, 116, 117, 118, 119, 120, 121.

Macmillan Publishing Co., Inc.
866 Third Avenue, New York, N.Y. 10022
Collier Macmillan Canada, Inc.

Library of Congress Cataloging in Publication Data

Herbert, Janice Summers.
  Oriental rugs.
  Bibliography: p.
  Includes index.
  1. Rugs, Oriental. I. Title.
NK2808.H52 1982   746.7′5   82-16219
ISBN 0-02-551130-0

10 9 8 7 6 5 4 3 2 1

Printed in the United States of America

CONTENTS

To my mother
Katherine Case Summers
with Love

ACKNOWLEDGMENTS

Many Oriental rug people freely gave their help and cooperation while I was compiling this manuscript. I am extremely grateful to:

Richard Amatulli (Amatulli Imports, New York)
Jacques Bodenmann (Mori S.A., Basel, Switzerland)
Abdolrahim Etessami (Etessami Brothers Oriental Rug Corp., New York)
Kamran Etessami (Etessami Brothers Oriental Rug Corp., New York)
Hans Felder (Oundjian, S.A., Zurich, Switzerland)
George O'Bannon (O'Bannon Oriental Carpets, Pittsburgh)
Larry Tadross (Oundjian, Inc., New York)

A special "thank-you" to my friends who so graciously offered their rugs to serve as illustrations; to Jacques Bodenmann, Bill Collins, Ted Herbert, and Richard LeNoir for their excellent photographs; and to my husband for providing the line drawings. My deepest appreciation to Helen Mills and Alexia Dorszynski for all of their hard work.

To my husband and son go my love and deep appreciation for understanding all the work involved in putting together this book.

Introduction to Oriental Rugs

FEW ART FORMS are surrounded with the aura or mystique that is associated with Oriental rugs. The entire subject has become romanticized to the extent that those interested in Oriental rugs have a great deal of difficulty separating fact from fancy. Those who undertake the study of Oriental rugs can quickly fall prey to an overwhelming and bewildering amount of highly technical information.

My aim is to provide a comprehensible review of the rugs most likely to be encountered in everyday life, and to give sound advice on the purchase and care of such rugs. Rather detailed treatment is given those rugs from Turkey, Iran, the Caucacus, and Turkestan; space limitations preclude more than a rather brief treatment of the rugs of China, India, and Pakistan. In another book,* these rugs, as well as those from Nepal and Romania, are given more detailed coverage. This book purposely excludes those pieces that most people are likely to encounter only in museums. For those who wish scholarly or detailed treatment of museum pieces, there are a number of excellent scholarly works available.

The term "Oriental rug" refers specifically to handmade (both knotted and woven) rugs; traditionally they have been woven in Iran, Turkey, the Caucasus regions of the Soviet Union, China, Turkestan (both east and west), India, and Pakistan. To be an Oriental rug, a rug MUST be hand-knotted or hand-woven. No rug that has been made by machine—even if it has an Oriental design—is a genuine Oriental rug. Nor does being made by hand qualify a rug to be a genuine Oriental rug—if it has been made by some method other than hand-knotting or hand-weaving. For example, hand-punched, hand-glued, or hand-sewn carpets, such as those made in the Philippines and in Hong Kong, are not genuine Oriental rugs.

An Oriental rug is an art form, but one need not be an expert or con-

---

* Janice Summers Herbert, *Affordable Oriental Rugs* (New York: Macmillan, 1980).

noisseur to appreciate and admire its beauty. As with any other art form, taste and preference are important; each rug is a uniquely individual expression of creativity—in a utilitarian form—and must be evaluated on its own merits. There are some general guides and procedures that one can follow in developing an informed evaluation and appreciation of Oriental rugs. We can group these as considerations of rug construction, design, origin, and evaluation; each of these is covered in a major section of this book.

As an art form, the Oriental rug retains the best of tradition, even while evolving to accommodate the tastes and needs of new generations. To further understand today's Oriental rugs, a brief review of the history of this art form may prove helpful.

Historical Overview

No one knows exactly when or where the first knotted-pile carpets were made. The oldest known example was found in 1947 in Siberia's Altai Mountains, in the Pazyryk Valley. This carpet, now known as the Pazyryk carpet, was found frozen in the burial mound of a fifth century B.C. Scythian prince.

This Pazyryk carpet is rather sophisticated in both design and weaving technique. Its central field has a panel-type design surrounded by five separate borders. One border contains reindeer figures; another, horsemen. Tied with the Turkish knot, the pile contains over two hundred knots per square inch. Such a carpet could only have been the product of a long history and tradition of weaving. The Pazyryk carpet exists only because of its having been frozen, preserved in ice.

We must assume that other carpets of similar age, as well as those of more recent vintage, simply deteriorated and crumbled to dust, leaving no trace for us. Indeed, our history of knotted-pile carpets consists largely of isolated carpet fragments, depiction in such contemporaneous media as paintings or sculpture, and ancient anecdotal references.

On a 2,500-year-old relief at Persepolis, an ambassador is depicted presenting gifts of rugs to the Persian king. Fifth- and sixth-century carpet fragments have been found along old caravan routes near Lou-lan in the Eastern Turkestan region of China.

The next era from which there is evidence by which to document the existence of weaving is the thirteenth century. Carpet fragments from this period have been found in mosques in Konya and Beyşehir, in present day Turkey. In his accounts of his travels in 1271–72 through what is now Turkey, Marco Polo referred to the carpets of Turkey as the finest and most beautiful in the world.

In the late fourteenth century, a little over a hundred years after Marco

Polo wrote of "Turkey carpets," knotted-pile carpets first appeared in European paintings. During the early fifteenth century, numerous paintings depicted the most holy of religious subjects, such as the Virgin, the Madonna and Child enthroned, as well as saints, placed upon knotted-pile carpets.

By the late fifteenth and early sixteenth centuries, numerous European paintings depicted Turkish carpets being hung from balastrades and used for floor and table coverings. Two artists, Hans Holbein the Younger, and Lorenzo Lotto, so prominently featured Oriental rugs with certain designs that their names have become associated with the rugs in which these designs appear. "Holbein" carpets feature one or more large-scaled octagonal motifs, or small octagonal motifs repeated in rows throughout the field. "Lotto" carpets are characterized by the use of repeated, highly stylized arabesques, so intricate that they give a lace-like appearance.

Holbein, Lotto, and other artists successfully applied their skills and talents, portraying carpets in such detail that the knots actually can be counted. By such pictorial evidence, these artists present an invaluable perspective on the use of Oriental rugs during that period.

Carpet weaving continued to flourish in Asia Minor under the Ottoman Turks. As their empire spread throughout southeastern Europe, so did the

PLATE 1: *Stone relief at Persepolis, showing the presentation of Oriental rugs to the Persian king.*

art of carpet weaving. Even today, knotted-pile carpets are still woven in Romania, Bulgaria, and Albania, and in parts of Yugoslavia and Greece.

The oldest Persian carpet fragment dates to the sixteenth century. However, there are Arab references to carpets of the Fars region of Persia in the ninth century. Persian carpets are pictured in miniatures of the fourteenth century from both Shiraz and northeastern Persia. The floors in the palace of Ghazan Khan in Tabriz were said to have been covered with carpets from Fars.

Under the Safavid rulers (1499–1722) the Persian arts as a whole had a renaissance. Of these rulers, Shah Abbas the Great (1587–1629) was the patron of the carpet industry. In 1590, Shah Abbas moved his capital to Isfahan, where he established workshops for the designers and weavers to create carpet masterpieces. After his death, the art of carpet-making declined steadily until the Afghan invasion in 1722, when the last remnants of the art were virtually destroyed. Very little carpet-making was done for the next 150 years.

During the last quarter of the nineteenth century, carpet-making was again reborn. Merchants from Tabriz set up looms for the making of carpets to meet the increasing interest and demand in Europe. Since that time, with only a few minor setbacks, carpet-making has had a steady increase in popularity and demand.

Carpet weaving on the Indian subcontinent began in the sixteenth century. The Moghul emperor, Akbar the Great, brought Persian weavers from Isfahan and Kashan to his courts in Lahore and Agra. He established royal workshops for the weaving of carpets. As a result of this Persian influence, the early Indian carpets were similar in both design and structure to those woven in Persia.

The Indian carpet industry declined as the Moghul dynasty came to an end, and with it the system of royal patronage. It was not until the mid-nineteenth century that the Indian carpet industry began to make a comeback. International interest had been piqued by an Indian carpet display

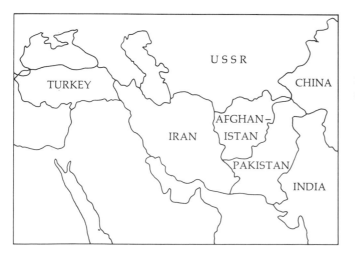

FIGURE 1: *RUG-WEAVING COUNTRIES OF THE WORLD*

at the Great London Exhibition of 1851. Foreign capital for expansion of the Indian carpet industry quickly followed. In the years since World War II, the Indian carpet industry has made great strides in improving the quality of workmanship.

Hand-knotted carpets emerged relatively late in Chinese history. Although theories abound on the origin of Chinese carpets, it is generally believed that hand-knotted carpets first appeared in Gansu and Ningshia, probably as a result of contact with nomads wandering eastward from Xinjiang and central Asia. Carpet weaving in China was done almost exclusively in the northwest provinces until the last quarter of the nineteenth century. Then, in 1871, Emperor T'ung Chih established schools for carpet weaving in Beijing, bringing lamas from the northwestern provinces to serve as teachers.

The early twentieth century saw great foreign interest for Chinese carpets. Weaving factories were quickly established to meet this demand. Beijing and Tianjin became the primary manufacturing centers for rugs woven largely for export; the designs of these rugs were, and still are, influenced to some extent by foreign tastes and market demands.

Currently, the carpet industry in China is operated by the China National Native Produce and Animal By-Products Import and Export Corporation. Carpets are made in weaving centers throughout the country in a wide variety of designs, color combinations, and structural characteristics.

Oriental Rugs Today

The Oriental carpet industry is constantly undergoing change. The availability of Oriental rugs on the world's markets is greatly affected by political instability and upheaval, industrial development, and changes in laws and tariffs. Situations internal to a country may affect the actual weaving and even the marketing of carpets once they have been completed.

Not surprisingly, worldwide inflation has affected the Oriental carpet industry. The costs of labor and raw materials used in the weaving of rugs have soared. Increased demand tends to make any product more expensive, and Oriental rugs are no exception. The carpet market adjusts to meet the changing patterns of the price and availability. Weaving centers take up the slack in production created by another center's decrease in production or popularity, offering new patterns and lower prices.

Although the structure of the marketplace and the variety of carpets it offers is changing constantly, the technique of weaving has remained relatively unchanged. Weaving is still the same labor-intensive process that it has been for centuries. Hundreds of thousands of individual knots are tied by hand to create a magnificent work of art.

2

Construction

ALL ORIENTAL RUGS are hand-knotted on a webbing formed by the warp and weft threads. Attached to the top and bottom of the loom, *warp* threads run vertically through the carpet. A strand of wool is tied to a pair of warp threads, forming a knot. The loose ends of the knots, which make up the body of the rug, are called *pile. Weft* threads run horizontally through the carpet and are used to secure the knots; one way to remember the difference between warp and weft threads is that wefts go from "weft" to right, not up and down.

Weaving Process

The weaver sits facing a loom upon which the warp threads are strung, while overhead are balls of colored yarn to be used in the rug. Reaching up, the weaver takes the end of a strand of spun wool, ties it across a pair of warp threads, and cuts free the end of the strand that is still attached to the ball of yarn. Tying and cutting the wool is done in one swift motion. So skilled are the weavers that, like the hands of a magician, their fingers move so deftly that the eye cannot follow them.

After each row of knots has been completed, one or more weft threads are woven in and out of each warp thread. To secure them firmly in place, the weft threads and knots are beaten down with a "comb." Any excess knotted yarn is trimmed with a large pair of scissors after each row of knots. (In some areas, this may be done after the carpet has been completed.) The weaver repeats this operation hundreds of times until the carpet has been completed.

Designs are formed by the arrangement of different-colored knotted yarns. The placement of each knot may be directed or specified in several different ways. The nomadic weaver, for example, is usually a woman,

PLATE 2: *Cartoon*

who weaves a carpet from patterns learned from her mother or from forms unique to her own tribe. The urban or semi-urban weaver may be a woman, a man, or even a child; this weaver has a section of a drawing (called a *cartoon* or *talim*) from which to work. These cartoons are usually drawn to scale with a single square on the piece of paper indicating each knot. The design is colored and cut in horizontal strips, then either placed in a plastic casing for protection or mounted on a board and varnished.

Carpets are finished in one of several different ways; the warp threads may be knotted and cut to form a fringe, a *kelim*, or a combination of the two. A *kelim* is a strip of cloth formed by weaving the weft threads back and forth through the warp threads. The selvedges, or the sides, of the carpet are secured and reinforced, generally by taking the last few warp threads and wrapping them tightly with an extra weft thread. Each weaving center has its own unique manner of securing the selvedge; these various processes will be discussed when the individual rugs are described.

Looms

There are two classifications of looms: the ground or horizontal loom and the upright or vertical loom. There are three types of vertical looms: the village type, the Tabriz type, and the roller beam type, all shown in Figure 2.

The *ground* or *horizontal loom* is the simplest of the looms. Because it is easily collapsed and moved from place to place, it is used by nomadic tribes, some seminomadic tribes, and villagers. The warp threads are fastened to upper and lower beams, which are held in place by stakes driven into the ground. When the nomads are ready to move, the stakes are removed, and the unfinished carpet is rolled around one of the beams. Once resettled, the carpet is unrolled, the stakes reset, and the weaving process begun again.

The simplest of the *vertical* looms is the *village type*. The weaver sits on a plank which is raised or lowered, always enabling the weaver to sit directly in front of the area of the carpet on which she is working. The

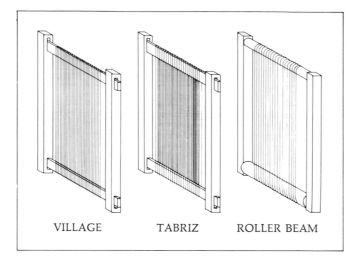

FIGURE 2: *LOOMS*

VILLAGE   TABRIZ   ROLLER BEAM

warp threads are attached to the upper and lower beams of a simple frame. Although the length of the carpet is usually only as long as the distance between the upper and lower beams, it is possible to make the carpet longer by a complicated process. In this procedure, the warp threads are loosened and the completed part of the rug is reattached to the lower beam. The warp threads are then retightened on the upper beam, and the weaving process is continued.

The *Tabriz type* of loom, so named because it originated in Tabriz, is a little more complicated than the village type. The warp threads pass in a continuous loop around the upper and lower beams. Slack in the warp threads is taken up by driving wedges in the space where the side supports meet the lower beam. The weavers do not have to be raised with this type of loom because, as the weaving process progresses, the rug is lowered down around the lower beam and up the back of the loom. The completed part of the carpet then can be easily inspected. With this type of loom, the carpet can be as long as twice the distance between the upper and lower beams (see Plate 3.)

The *roller beam type* is the most advanced of the looms. The warp threads are wound around the upper beam, leaving the ends attached to the lower beam. As the weaving progresses, the warp threads are unwound from the upper beam and the finished part of the carpet is rolled around the lower beam. It is easy to weave carpets of any length on this loom. In addition, the tension of the warps is adjusted by rotating the beams, producing a straighter carpet. Looms of this type are used in Kerman.

PLATE 3: *Tabriz weavers at loom*

Materials

Cotton and wool are the most important materials used in the creation of Oriental rugs. Silk is also used, though its expense limits its use. The use of cotton and wool depends largely on their availability. The warp and weft threads of most Persian and Chinese rugs are cotton, whereas those of most Caucasian and Turkoman rugs are wool. The pile of Oriental rugs is generally wool. The exception to the rule is the silk rug; warp, weft, and pile are all made of silk. Other carpets are woven with a wool pile on silk warp and weft threads; still others have a silk pile and cotton warp and weft threads.

Cotton is a better fiber for the warp and weft threads than wool. It does not possess the elastic tendencies of wool and knots can be tied tighter to a cotton warp, yielding a more closely woven carpet. Rugs made with a cotton warp and weft are also heavier than those made of wool; as a result they lie flatter on the floor and will not "walk" or "creep." Silk is the strongest fiber used for warp threads because of its tensile strength. The most finely knotted rugs are woven with silk warp threads.

Wools vary greatly from region to region. Many different factors affect texture, color, quality, and durability, including breed of sheep, climate, and time of year in which the wool is shorn (either fall or spring). For example, sheep raised in the mountain areas have heavier and thicker wool than sheep raised in the desert. Because wools vary so greatly, the characteristics will be discussed with each type of rug.

Silk has been used in the making of carpets since the earliest of times. Very few silk rugs are woven today for several reasons. First, the silk itself is very expensive; and second, because silk pile does not wear particularly well, its use has been restricted largely to rugs for decorative purposes, such as wall hangings.

PLATE 4: *Tying knot with Tabriz hook*

In recent years, mercerized cotton has been developed which, when woven in a rug, resembles silk so closely that it is hard to tell the difference. The use of mercerized cotton is common in Turkish and some Turkoman rugs, and these rugs have often been represented to unsuspecting buyers as silk. Murray Eiland[1] suggests the best way to tell the difference is to wet a small portion of the rug; the wet mercerized cotton will feel more like ordinary cotton, and the silk rug will retain its silky feel.

Goat's hair and camel's hair are occasionally encountered in Oriental rugs. The Qashqai, Balouchi, and Afghans use goat's hair for selvedges and, on occasion, for warp and weft threads. Balouchis quite often used camel's hair as the ground for their Tree-of-life prayer rugs.[2] Many people believe that the caramel-colored wool found in Hamadan and Kurd rugs is camel's hair. Although it was occasionally used, most caramel- or "camel"-colored wool is sheep's wool that has been dyed with walnut husks. Camel's hair possesses a definite odor when wet.

There is a practice in which the wool of butchered sheep ("skin" or "dead" wool) is used. The animal skin is submerged in a caustic solution which allows the wool to be easily scraped from the skin. This process, however, weakens the woolen fibers, and rugs made with this wool will wear much faster than those made with wool shorn from living sheep. Also, skin wool takes dyes poorly and gives a carpet a dull and lusterless appearance. With experience, skin wool can be readily detected; skin wool feels comparatively coarse and bristly to the touch.

---

[1] Murray Eiland, *Oriental Rugs: A Comprehensive Guide* (Greenwich, Conn.: New York Graphic Society, Ltd., 1973), p. 25.

[2] George O'Bannon, personal correspondence, Nov. 3, 1980.

Knots

The spun wool may be tied to the warp threads in two different ways, either by a Turkish (Ghiordes) or a Persian (Senna) knot (see Figure 3). Though the tying technique of these types of knots may vary slightly from region to region, the end result is the same.

FIGURE 3: *KNOTS*

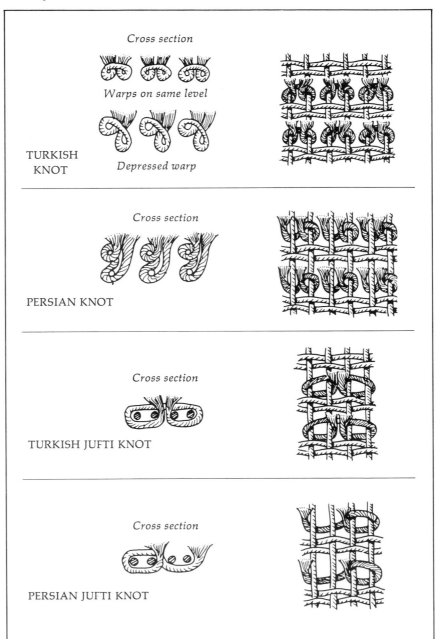

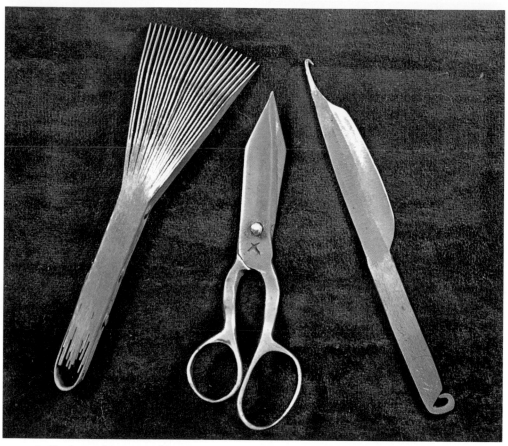

PLATE 6: *Tools used in rugmaking*

The nomenclature is somewhat confusing and can be misleading. For example, some authors refer to the Persian knot as the Senna knot (named after the ancient town of Senna). However, the rugs made in Senna are woven with the Turkish knot and never with the Senna knot. The Turkish knot is sometimes called the Ghiordes knot, named for the small town of Ghiordes in the western Anatolian plateau of Turkey. Yet this knot is used not only in Ghiordes, but in almost all of Turkey, in all of Caucasia, and in many tribal and village areas of Iran. Turks and Turki-speaking peoples usually employ the Turkish knot, regardless of the tribe's location. Persian and Farsi-speaking peoples weave with the Persian knot.

The *Turkish knot* is a strand of wool that encircles two warp threads, with the loose ends drawn tightly between the two warps. This is the easiest knot to tie, but also the coarsest.

The *Persian knot* is a strand of wool that encircles one warp thread and winds loosely around the other. One loose end is pulled through the two warp threads, while the other emerges outside of the paired warps. Although the more difficult of the two types to tie, the Persian knot gives a more clearly defined pattern and a more tightly woven rug.

The *jufti,* or "false," knot is simply a Turkish or Persian knot tied to four warp threads instead of two. The use of the *jufti* knot spread throughout the carpet-weaving industry in epidemic proportions after World War II. By using this knot, the weaver was able to tie half as many knots as would normally be required if he used the Turkish or Persian knot. Since four warp threads are used instead of two, a carpet may be woven with half the number of knots, in half the time. Pile density is halved, yielding a carpet that is much less resistant to wear. The widespread use of the *jufti* was curbed during the 1960s and it is not the threat to the carpet industry that it once was.

Dyes

The dyeing process is a delicate and complicated one. The procedure may vary slightly, depending on the substance used in making the dye. Basically, the wool is chemically treated to make it more receptive to the dye and then submerged in a vat full of dye. The length of time the wool stays in the vat depends upon the type of dye and the hue desired, and may last as long as a few hours to a few days. When the desired color has been attained, the wool is removed and spread in the sun to dry.

There are three types of dyes that have been used in the dyeing of Oriental rugs: natural vegetable and animal, aniline, and chrome. Aniline and chrome are synthetic dyes.

NATURAL VEGETABLE AND ANIMAL DYES

Making and using the natural vegetable dyes is time-consuming and can be quite expensive. The colors are derived from a number of different sources:

madder red—root of the madder plant
cochineal red—cochineal insect
yellow—weld, vine leaves, or pomegranate peel
brown—walnut shells or oak bark
orange—henna leaves
blue—indigo plant
green—combination of weld and indigo

In older rugs there is often a slight change of color which will run horizontally through the field of the carpet. This is called an *abrash.* It occurs because the yarn is sometimes dyed in small batches, and because, especially with vegetable dyes, it is hard to obtain an exact match in color between different dye lots. The *abrash* is created when the weaver begins using yarn from a dye lot that does not exactly match the dye lot previously employed. This is not objectionable in itself and does not affect the quality of the rug.

ANILINE DYES

The use of aniline dyes was introduced to the carpet industry in the latter half of the nineteenth century. Being easier and cheaper to use, these dyes were adopted all too readily. They were usually strongly acidic, which destroyed the natural oil in the wool, thus weakening the pile and causing it to wear rapidly. The colors not only faded when exposed to sunlight, but ran when washed. These dyes damaged the rug industry so severely that the Persian government passed laws in the 1890s prohibiting their importation and use. Inferior chemical dyes are still used in some bazaar-quality Turkish rugs. Aniline-dyed rugs are easily recognized by their faded colors; the back is much brighter than the sunlight-faded front.

CHROME DYES

Most rugs are now dyed with what are commonly referred to as "chrome dyes," synthetic dyes treated with potassium bichromate. In contrast to the natural dyes, chrome dyes are much simpler to prepare and their dye lots easier to match. These dyes provide a wider variety of shades, are colorfast, and will not fade when exposed to sunlight or washed with water or an alkaline solution. The natural oils of the wool are not removed by the dyes, so the wearing qualities of the rug are not impaired.

The major complaint about chrome dyes has been that their colors are harsher than the mellow hues of natural dyes, a problem which has been corrected by the use of a light chemical wash. Too often the imperfections of natural dyes are forgotten. For example, oak bark, which was used to make black and brown dyes, contained iron salts which weakened woolen fibers and caused them to wear rapidly.

The Wash

Most Oriental rugs are given a light chemical wash before being exported. This wash simply enhances the richness of the rug and does not affect its durability.

CHEMICAL WASH

A luster, or sheen, may be given a carpet by the chemical wash. The type of wool used for the pile and the chemical concentration of the wash are two factors that affect the amount of luster imparted. Wools vary from region to region; certain wools are more receptive to the chemical wash, gaining a more lustrous appearance than others.

"ANTIQUE" WASH

An "antique" wash has been developed to give new rugs an old look. This is a rather heavy chemical wash which tones down the colors and gives the impression of an antique rug. Rugs with an antique wash can be detected by splitting the pile and examining its base. The top of the pile will have a drabber, more muted color than the base. The wash also gives the fringes a brownish cast.

WASHED AND PAINTED

For several decades (1920 to 1940), the colors of new Persian rugs were thought to be too bright for the expanding American market. Rugs were given a rather heavy chemical wash to tone down what Americans considered harsh colors, such as bright red. While the heavy wash did subdue the colors, it also removed the natural oils from the woolen pile fibers, greatly reducing the rug's life span. Over a period of time, the heavy wash also destroyed the warp and weft threads. When folded, the rug's foundation would actually crack and break.

Washing reduced the brilliant color contrasts within a rug, turning the red ground into a drab, muted pinkish rose. Since the darker reds, especially maroon, were particularly appealing to American tastes, a "painting" process was initiated. The washed ground color was colored or "painted" with a hand-applied dye. Another process was then necessary to add the desired luster or sheen to the rug. Almost all Sarouks, as well as some Dergazines and Lillihans imported during this period, were both washed and painted.

3

Design

THE DESIGNS AND VARIATIONS in Oriental rugs are so numerous that it would be impossible to describe them all. These variations in design occur in the two main parts of the rug: the *field* (or *ground*) and the *borders*, which frame the interior (the field of the carpet). Designs fall into two different categories: curvilinear and rectilinear (see Plates 7 and 8). *Curvilinear* designs have floral motifs and patterns, with curved outlines and tendrils; *rectilinear* designs have geometric or angular motifs and patterns. Both of these categories are classified by the type of design or pattern which occupies the field: medallion, repeated motif, all-over, and prayer.

Medallion

The medallion rug will have a field which is dominated by a central medallion or by several medallions. The field surrounding the medallion may be open (empty), filled, or semiopen (small motifs scattered throughout the field).

Repeated Motif

In a repeated design, the central field is filled with multiple rows of the same motif. Among the repeated designs are the Mina Khani, Guli Henna, Herati, Zil-i-soltan, Boteh, and Gul patterns.

MINA KHANI

The Mina Khani design is comprised of repeated floral motifs, each of which is surrounded by four similar smaller flowers, joined in turn by

PLATE 7: *RECTILINEAR (Tabriz)*   PLATE 8: *CURVILINEAR (Tabriz)*

vines to form a diamond arrangement. The design is found in older Bijars, occasionally in Hamadans and Kurds, and quite often in the Veramin (see Figure 4).

GULI HENNA

Guli Henna (henna flower) has small yellow plantlike motifs which resemble stalks with many flowers and leaves, and are set in rows; each motif is contained within a diamond-shaped bouquet. This pattern is most often used in older rugs from the Hamadan and the Sultanabad areas (see Figure 4).

HERATI

The Herati pattern is the design used most often in the Persian rugs. It consists of a rosette surrounded by four leaves or "fish" and generally, though not necessarily, found inside a diamond shape ("lozenge"). Bijar, Ferahan, and Hamadan weave the Herati design with the diamond; Khurasan weaves it without the diamond (see Figure 4).

26

| HERATI | ZIL-I-SOLTAN | MINA KHANI | GULI HENNA |

FIGURE 4: *REPEATED MOTIFS*

ZIL-I-SOLTAN

The Zil-i-soltan design is made up of multiple rows of repeated motifs, each of which resembles a vase of roses. This design is found more frequently in Qum and Abadeh; however, it is not restricted to those areas (see Figure 4).

BOTEH

The Boteh (paisley) design contains multiple rows of repeated *botehs* (pine cones or pears). It is probably the most widespread pattern, found in Persian, Caucasian, and some Turkoman rugs. Botehs come in many different forms and shapes, some of which are illustrated in Plates 9–14.

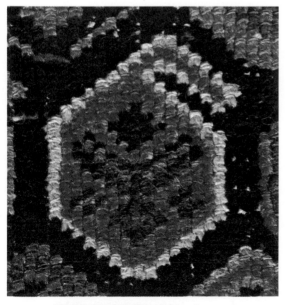

PLATE 9: *PERSIAN BOTEH (Shiraz)*

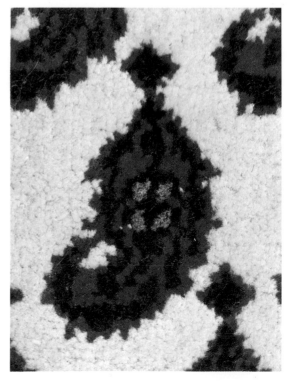

PLATE 10: *PERSIAN BOTEH (Tabriz)*

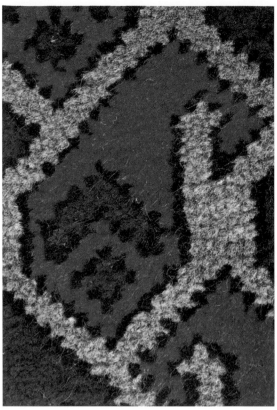

PLATE 11: *PERSIAN BOTEH (Senna)*

PLATE 12: *BALOUCH BOTEH*

PLATE 13: *BOTEH (Seraband)*

PLATE 14: *CAUCASIAN BOTEH (Shirvan)*

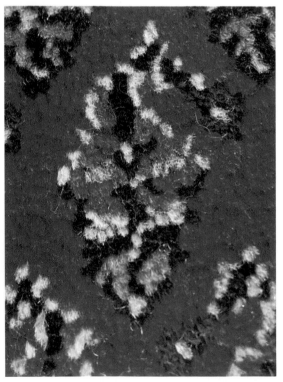

PLATE 15: *GUL (Yomud)*

GUL

The Gul (Persian for "flower") is a distinctive rectilinear emblem unique to each Turkoman tribe (see Chapter 6, Figure 20). These multiple identical *guls* are arranged in rows.

All-Over Design

The all-over design has a field filled with a pattern which has neither a "repeated" nor a regimented form. An all-over design will have very little repetition and a large-scale pattern which fills the field. In contrast, the "repeated" design fills the field with multiple rows of a single motif. Examples of the all-over designs are Shah Abbas, Garden (or Hunting), Tree (or Vase), Panel, and Picture (see Plates 16–19).

SHAH ABBAS

The Shah Abbas pattern (named for the patron of carpet-making, Shah Abbas the Great) is floral in character. The field is filled with palmettes and vases, which are interspersed within an intricate network of tendrils. The Shah Abbas pattern is woven often in Isfahan, Kashan, and Tabriz and occasionally in other carpet-weaving areas.

PLATE 16: *GARDEN DESIGN (Qum)*   PLATE 17: *SHAH ABBAS DESIGN (Qum)*

GARDEN OR HUNTING

The Garden or Hunting pattern represents a nature scene in which combinations of trees, flowers, animals, and birds, and human figures fill the field. The Hunting design is a variation of the Garden pattern, with the addition of hunters (usually with bow and arrow). The Garden pattern is woven in Qum as well as in other weaving centers; the Hunting pattern is most often associated with Tabriz.

TREE OR VASE

The Tree or Vase pattern contains a vase or tree centered at the base of the field from which emanate tendrils or branches; these, with flowers and leaves, fill the field. The Tree-of-life and the Weeping Willow (*Bid Majnūm*), examples of the tree pattern, are found in the carpets of Hamadan, and occasionally in those of Tabriz and Bijar. Vase patterns are woven most often in the carpets of Kashan.

PANEL DESIGN

Panel design carpets are easily recognized by the rectangular compartments ("panels") into which the field is divided. Each compartment encloses

30

PLATE 18: *TREE OR VASE DESIGN (Qum)*   PLATE 19: *PANEL DESIGN (Tabriz)*

one of a variety of motifs: flowers, trees, *boteh*, palmettes, and so on. The design was adopted from the matrix formed by irrigation channels in Persian gardens. Excellent examples of this design are woven in Tabriz and Qum.

PICTURE CARPETS

Picture carpets are those in which portraits or scenes are woven. Like a painting, picture carpets endeavor to realistically portray a specific person, still life, or landscape. Tapestry-like rugs with scenic landscapes are woven in China. In Iran, China, and Pakistan, carpets are woven with scenes depicting myths, legends, and religious themes. Portrait carpets are also woven depicting the likenesses of political or religious leaders.

Prayer Rugs

Prayer rugs are easily identified by the prayer niche (*mihrab*) or arch present (see Plate 20). The arch may be either geometric or curvilinear; the

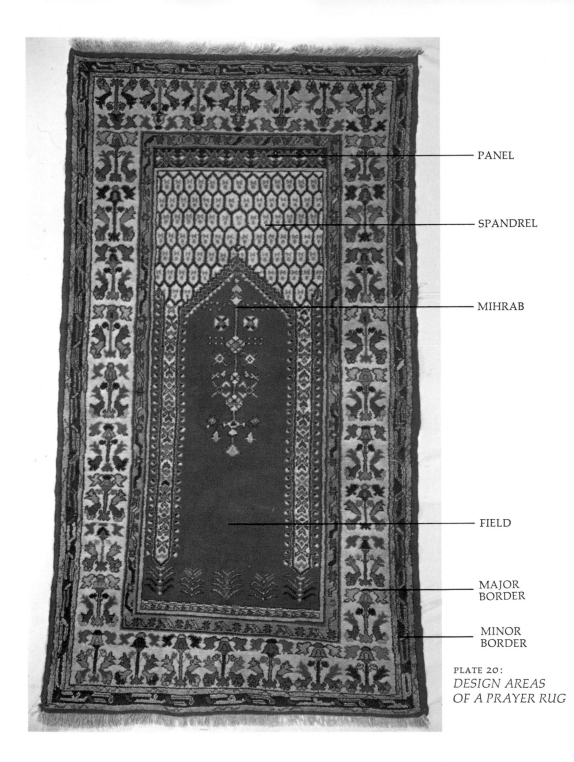

PANEL

SPANDREL

MIHRAB

FIELD

MAJOR
BORDER

MINOR
BORDER

PLATE 20:
*DESIGN AREAS
OF A PRAYER RUG*

prayer niche may be empty or filled with motifs common to the area where the rug was woven. Prayer rugs have been woven throughout Turkey, Iran, the Caucasus, and Turkestan. Copies of traditional patterns are woven in Pakistán, India, and Romania.

Rugs with multiple *mihrabs*, referred to as *saffs*, traditionally have been woven in Eastern Turkestan (Xinjiang) and Turkey. Copies of Turkish *saffs* are also woven in Pakistan.

Borders

A series of borders or "frames" surround and set off the interior and major attraction of the carpet, its ground or field. Just as the field designs and motifs vary, the borders also differ. The standard arrangement is from three to seven borders, with a few exceptions. (Kerman, for example, weaves an Aubusson-type border; see Plate 59.) Borders are not limited to

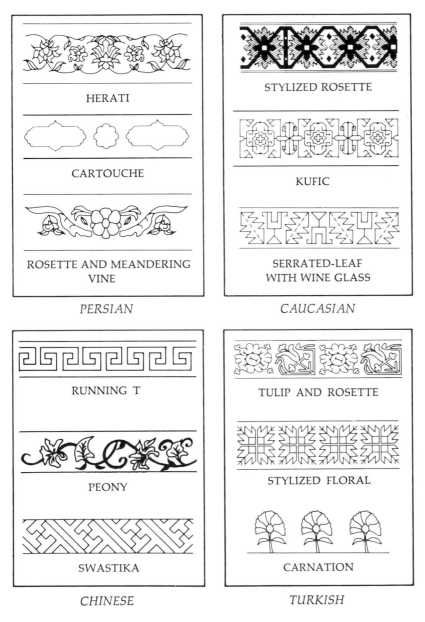

FIGURE 5: *MAJOR BORDER DESIGNS*

HERATI

CARTOUCHE

ROSETTE AND MEANDERING VINE

PERSIAN

STYLIZED ROSETTE

KUFIC

SERRATED-LEAF WITH WINE GLASS

CAUCASIAN

RUNNING T

PEONY

SWASTIKA

CHINESE

TULIP AND ROSETTE

STYLIZED FLORAL

CARNATION

TURKISH

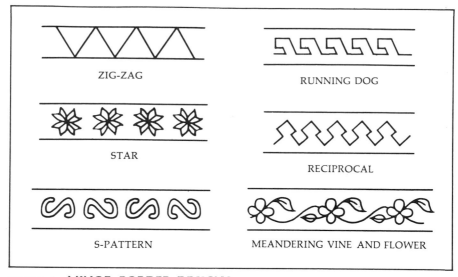

FIGURE 6: *MINOR BORDER DESIGNS*

particular types of rugs, designs, or origin. Border designs have been freely borrowed, adopted, and adapted for each area's own use. (The Herati border used in the Herez rugs is stylized and geometric, as contrasted to the more intricate floral form of the Herati used in the rugs of Isfahan.) The number of borders varies from rug to rug, depending on its size, design, and origin. Generally, there is a single main border (*Ara-Khachi*), flanked by matching smaller borders (*Bala-Khachi*). The minor borders may be separated from the major borders by lines or by even smaller minor borders.

Major border designs that are widely used in Persian rugs are the Herati, a series of palmettes connected by flowering vines; cartouche, cloudlike enclosures containing poetic inscriptions or proverbs; *boteh*, which are interspersed with vines; and animal, or hunting, figures. In Caucasian and Turkish rugs major borders are more geometric, as in the stylized rosette, Kufic, and the serrated-leaf. (See Figure 5.)

Examples of minor borders found in Persian, Caucasian, and Turkish rugs are zig-zag, reciprocal, running dog, S-pattern, meandering vine and flower, and star (see Figure 6).

Dates

Occasionally dates are woven into Oriental rugs. The numerals are usually in Persian script and are easily translated into the western form (see Figure 7). With a few exceptions, dates are based on the Muhammedan calendar, which begins with the Hegira, Muhammed's flight from Mecca on July 16, A.D. 622. The Moslem calendar, based on the lunar year, is about one-third shorter than the solar-year calendar used in Europe and the western hemisphere.

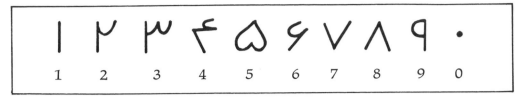

1	2	3	4	5	6	7	8	9	0

FIGURE 7: *NUMERICAL SIGNS*

Converting the Persian numerals to the equivalent western date is complicated by the existence of three different dating practices. First, the lunar-based Moslem calendar is typically the basis for dates on antique and semi-antique rugs. Second, since the early 1920s scattered instances of solar-based dates in Persian numerals—still based on the Moslem calendar—have appeared. Third, from 1971 to 1978, the Iranian calendar was based on the founding of the Persian Empire 2,500 years ago; the calendar was also converted from the lunar to the solar year, with the New Year (*Now Ruz*) beginning on March 21. After the Iranian Revolution in 1979, the standard lunar-based Moslem calendar was restored.

The use of different dating practices can be confusing, and at times several must be tried. Without strong evidence that one particular method has been used, it is sensible to apply the different formulas in turn, choosing the date that is most consistent with such factors as condition, type of dyes, materials, and design.*

CONVERSION PROCEDURES

To convert the *lunar-based Moslem date,* a simple mathematical procedure is necessary (see Figure 8). Converting the *solar-based Moslem date* requires only the addition of 622 to obtain its western equivalent.

To convert the 1971–78 *Iranian calendar dates,* one must subtract 560 from the date. Occasionally, the Muhammedan date will have only three numbers, the first numeral (1) having been omitted. Woven dates have been known to have been altered; in such cases the second digit, usually a

---

* As an alternative to the complicated process of converting from the lunar-based Moslem calendar, add 585 to the date, e.g., 1312 + 585 = 1897. This is accurate to within five years of the actual date and is close enough for a quick estimate.

FIGURE 8: *CONVERTING MOSLEM DATES*

	convert to equivalent	1322
	divide the date by 33	1322 ÷ 33 = 40
	subtract the quotient from the year	1322 − 40 = 1282
	add 622	1282 + 622 = 1904

3, is changed to a 2. This is more prevalent in Turkoman carpets than in the Persian or Caucasian carpets.

A woven date can be helpful in establishing vintage. This might increase the asking price of an antique or semi-antique carpet because it eliminates some uncertainty regarding the rug's age. Dates woven into new carpets do not affect production costs or wholesale prices, and should not increase retail price.

Symbols and Myths

Over the years many different designs and motifs have been used in Oriental rugs. Some have had special symbolic significance attributed to them. The mystique of Oriental rugs owes a lot to the tales and fables that have been built up around the different design elements.

Even though designs, motifs, and colors have little or no particular significance today, there are traditional interpretations associated with them. Symbols and colors with deep religious meaning for one group or sect may have a completely different meaning for another. For example, a human or animal figure was rarely woven into a carpet made by Sunnite Moslems; they were very strict in their interpretation of the Koran law forbidding the use of figures that represent living creatures. By contrast, the Shi'ite Moslems freely used figures of humans and animals in their carpets.

The interpretations most often associated with the various colors and motifs are shown in Figures 9 and 10.

For the past hundred years, market demand has determined which designs and motifs have been woven. A nomadic or a seminomadic weaver would tend to weave either what she sees, translating it into characteristic formats, or what she has been taught. The village weaver, on the other hand, typically weaves what is ordered, according to the cartoon.

Each rug is a separate work of art and should be considered individually. Its value does not lie in the meaning of its motifs, but in the special feeling it arouses in the proud possessor.

FIGURE 9: *TRADITIONAL COLOR INTERPRETATIONS*

COLOR	INTERPRETATION	COLOR	INTERPRETATION
RED	*Happiness, Joy*	BLACK	*Destruction*
BLUE	*Solitude, Truth*	ORANGE	*Devotion, Piety*
WHITE	*Purity, Peace, Grief*	YELLOW	*Power, Glory*
BROWN	*Fertility*	GREEN	*Paradise, "Prophet's Color," Sacred Color*

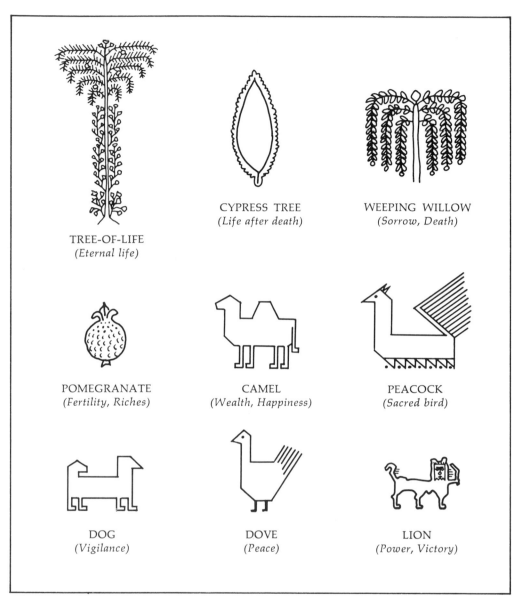

TREE-OF-LIFE
(Eternal life)

CYPRESS TREE
(Life after death)

WEEPING WILLOW
(Sorrow, Death)

POMEGRANATE
(Fertility, Riches)

CAMEL
(Wealth, Happiness)

PEACOCK
(Sacred bird)

DOG
(Vigilance)

DOVE
(Peace)

LION
(Power, Victory)

FIGURE 10: *TRADITIONAL INTERPRETATION OF MOTIFS*

4

Persian (Iranian) Rugs

IRAN IS A COUNTRY rich in history and tradition which can be traced back over 2,500 years to the ancient Persian Empire. Known as Persia until 1935, Iran has for many centuries been noted for weaving the world's finest and most beautiful rugs.

Situated on a plateau in southwest Asia, Iran is almost completely surrounded by mountains. The land area is about two and a half times that of the state of Texas. For hundreds of years Iran was basically an agricultural nation; the discovery of vast oil deposits in the early 1900s provided the basis for industrial and economic development. However, after the Iranian Revolution in 1979, economic and industrial policies changed.

The majority of Iranians are of Aryan origin, part of the Indo-European race; 90 percent are Moslems. Many different ethnic groups also abide in Iran, including Kurds, Armenians, Arabs, and Balouchis, each maintaining its own heritage, traditions, and culture. These ethnic groups and tribes weave rugs that reflect the uniqueness and character of the weaver and his environs.

Even though the vast majority of Iranians are settled in towns and villages, some tribes still cling to the nomadic way of life. Carpets woven by nomads are generally labeled with the tribal name, such as Qashqai and Afshar; those made by settled (residing in a town or village) weavers are named for the town in which they are woven or where they were marketed, such as Kerman and Hamadan. Figure 11 shows the major weaving centers of Iran.

When translated into English, Iranian names often appear with several different spellings, a difficulty caused by the phonetic translation from Farsi (the modern Persian language) to English. As pronunciation is not always obvious, a Pronunciation Guide is provided in Appendix II (p. 170). Alternate spellings are noted under specific rug headings in the text.

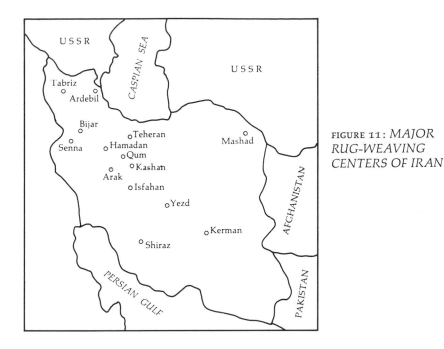

FIGURE 11: *MAJOR RUG-WEAVING CENTERS OF IRAN*

TABRIZ

KNOT:	*Turkish*
WARP:	*thick cotton*
WEFT:	*cotton, double*
PILE:	*coarse, heavy wool*
FRINGE:	*plain or knotted at both ends*
SELVEDGE:	*several warp threads overcast with wool*

It was in Tabriz that carpets were first woven strictly for export. In the mid-nineteenth century, the Tabrizi merchants collected and sent to Europe, via Istanbul, old and used carpets from homes and other sources. These carpets became so popular that demand soon exceeded the supply. Acknowledging the dwindling availability of rugs and foreseeing their eventual exhaustion, the enterprising Tabrizi merchants set up carpet-weaving houses or factories.

The city of Tabriz is located in northwestern Iran, near the Russian and Turkish borders (see Figure 12). For centuries it has been a commercial center because of its location at the juncture of major trade routes to the Far East and southern Persia.

The weavers of Tabriz are among the most skilled in Iran. They use a tool that enables the weaver to tie a knot a second. The *Tabriz hook* (see Plate 6) consists of a knife, similar to that used in the other weaving centers, at the tip of which is a small hook. This unique implement enables

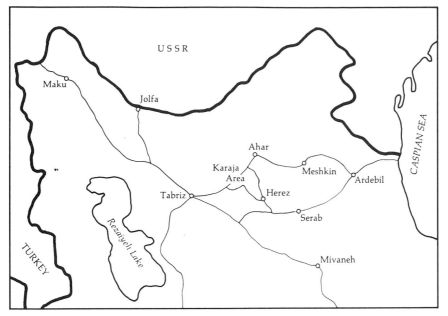

FIGURE 12: *AZERBAIJAN REGION*

the weaver to isolate a pair of warp threads, loop a strand of wool around the warps, then cut the strand free, all in one continuous motion.

Carpets woven in Tabriz can vary widely in quality, ranging from some of the world's finest carpets to a poor, "bazaar" quality. There are two main types of Tabriz carpets that one is likely to encounter, the "Fine" Tabriz and the "Taba Tabae" Tabriz, both of excellent quality.

The "Fine" Tabriz has been woven primarily for the European markets. These carpets are tightly woven, with pile trimmed quite short; designs are finely and crisply executed. Ground colors are deep, rich shades, usually of red or blue. Common designs include the Shah Abbas, Medallion, Picture, and Zil-i-soltan.

The "Taba Tabae" Tabrizes were designed to appeal to North American tastes and pocketbooks. These reasonably priced carpets were the most popular Persian rugs in the United States during the decade of the 1970s. The "Taba Tabae" is woven on a foundation of thick cotton warp and weft threads. The pile is heavy, thick wool, medium in length. Taba Tabaes are woven in popular earth tones of brown, gold, green, ivory, blue, and pastel colors. The most common designs are the Hunting, Garden, Medallion, and Herati designs. The Hunting design, in particular, has become so strongly associated with Tabriz that Hunting-design rugs woven in India and Romania are called "Indo-Tabriz" and "Romanian Tabriz" respectively.

The rugs of Tabriz are available in almost any size, from small mats and runners to the large gallery size. Round carpets are also woven in Tabriz.

PLATE 21: *TABRIZ (Medallion Design), 3 ft. 7 in. by 5 ft. 3 in.
Courtesy of Capt. and Mrs. George Gipe*

PLATE 22: *TABRIZ*
(Hunting Design)
2 ft. 8 in.
by 2 ft. 9 in.

PLATE 23: *TABRIZ (Zil-i-soltan Design) 2 ft. by 3 ft. 1 in.*
Courtesy of Mrs. Russell Summers

HEREZ *(Heriz)*

KNOT: *Turkish*
WARP: *cotton*
WEFT: *cotton, double, usually dyed light blue*
PILE: *medium; heavy, good-quality wool*
FRINGE: *plain or knotted fringe at both ends*
SELVEDGE: *overcast with wool*

The Herez area lies forty miles east of Tabriz, and consists of about thirty small villages, the more important of which are Herez, Ahar, Gorevan, and Meriban. The villages weave essentially the same design (see Plates 24 and 25), the only major difference being in quality: some Herez-area rugs are superior to others. Although the quality of weaving is not associated with specific villages, the names of the villages are used to denote the various grades of Herez-area rugs. The best of the Herez-area rugs is the *Herez;* those in the middle quality range are called *Meriban* or *Ahar.* The inferior grade, called *Gorevan,* was an excellent carpet at the turn of the century, but its quality began to deteriorate after World War I.

PLATE 24: *HEREZ*
3 ft. by 5 ft.
*Courtesy of Mr. and
Mrs. George Sinkinson*

PLATE 25: *AHAR*
2 ft. 9 in. by 3 ft. 8 in.
Courtesy of Mr. and
Mrs. Richard LeNoir

Serapi is the name given by some rug dealers to older Herez-quality rugs. This labeling is incorrect and misleading. No village by that name exists in Iran, and the term is a corruption of Serab, a small village approximately halfway between Tabriz and Ardebil. Ninety percent of the rugs woven in Serab are runners, and show few similarities to the rugs of Herez in size or design.

Herez-area rugs are imported under their correct quality classification. When retailed, however, these rugs are often lumped together under the single label of "Herez."

Herez rugs are similar to those of Tabriz in design, both Herez and Tabriz weavers using the same medallion-and-corner cartoons. In Herez rugs the design is interpreted in a rectilinear fashion; in Tabriz, in a curvilinear fashion. Although they are more coarsely woven than the rugs of Tabriz, Herez rugs are very durable and will take heavy traffic. Most of the rugs were woven in the 8 by 10 feet to 10 by 14 feet sizes; however, smaller rugs are occasionally found.

KARAJA *(Karadja)*

KNOT:	*Turkish*
WARP:	*cotton*
WEFT:	*cotton, single*
PILE:	*medium long, good-quality wool*
FRINGE:	*knotted at both ends*
SELVEDGE:	*several warp threads overcast with cotton or wool*

The rugs of Karaja are woven in the small town of Karaja and in several smaller surrounding villages.

Their distinctive geometric design of three medallions makes the Karaja an easily identifiable rug (see Plate 26). The center medallion is dark blue, and the other two either cream or green. The field is usually madder red with a navy-blue main border; however, these colors are often reversed. Runners and the larger rugs have the same medallion motifs, but are sequenced to fill the field.

Most of the rugs woven are either smaller sizes or runners. Large sizes are made, but room-size rugs are rather uncommon.

PLATE 26: *KARAJA*
1 ft. 9 in. by 2 ft. 8 in.

45

ARDEBIL *(Ardabil)*

KNOT: *Turkish*

WARP: *cotton (wool in older rugs)*

WEFT: *cotton (wool in older rugs)*

PILE: *short, good-quality wool*

FRINGE: *knotted at both ends*

SELVEDGE: *several warp threads overcast with wool (cotton in newer rugs)*

Carpets woven in Ardebil, which is located just twenty miles south of the southernmost reaches of the Caucasus region, reflect a strong Caucasian influence (see Plate 27). A design with three notched, diamond-shaped medallions is most often used. The field may be filled with a variety of small geometric motifs and shapes: stars, rosettes, and human and animal figures. Other designs resemble those of the older Shirvans and Kubas. A wide range of colors are used; cream, rust, and green are commonly used in the field, although reds, blues, and yellows are also found. The Ardebils are finely woven with good-quality wool in sizes ranging from small mats to room-size carpets.

PLATE 27: *ARDEBIL, 3 ft. by 4 ft. 8 in. Courtesy of Mrs. Russell Summers*

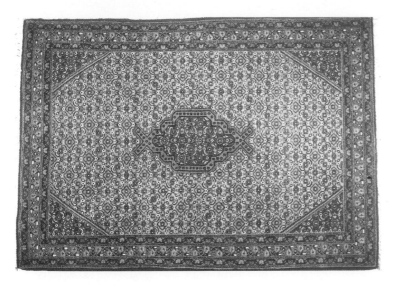

SENNABAFF

KNOT:	*Persian*
WARP:	*cotton*
WEFT:	*cotton*
PILE:	*medium short, excellent-quality wool*
FRINGE:	*knotted at both ends*
SELVEDGE:	*overcast with wool*

Rugs labeled as Sennabaff are woven in and around the town of Ardebil. Sennabaffs take their name from the manner in which they are woven. Instead of the Ghiordes (Turkish) knot usually woven in Ardebil and the Azerbadjian region, Sennabaff weavers employ the Senna (Persian) knot. *Baff* is the Persian word for knot, thus the carpet is named for its Senna-knotting technique.

The Herati design, reminiscent of antique Senna carpets (see p. 51), is always used. Common design variations involve the use of a central medallion and corner medallions, always with the Herati design filling the rest of the field. Regardless of whether or not a central medallion appears, a Sennabaff may—or may not—have corner medallions. The colors in Sennabaff carpets are soft; shades of blue, cream, rust, and coral are used. Sennabaffs are woven in virtually all sizes.

Excellent-quality wool is used in the carpets of Sennabaff. They are more tightly woven than Ardebils; therefore their pile is thicker and denser. Sennabaffs are an excellent-quality carpet, with an ability to withstand wear quite well.

PLATE 29: *MESHKIN*
5 ft. 4 in. by 8 ft. 2 in.
Courtesy of Mr. and
Mrs. Richard LeNoir

MESHKIN

KNOT:	*Turkish*
WARP:	*wool or cotton*
WEFT:	*wool or cotton*
PILE:	*medium to medium long*
FRINGE:	*knotted at both ends*
SELVEDGE:	*overcast with wool*

Meshkin is about fifty miles northwest of Ardebil, just south of the Caucasus border. The designs of Meshkin, like those of Ardebil, resemble those of the older Caucasian rugs, and the bold geometric medallions used are similar to those of Kazak (see Plate 29). The colors used are more muted than the Ardebils, blues and earth tones of gold and brown. In addition, the weave is much coarser and the pile longer than that of Ardebil. All sizes are woven, from mats to room-sizes.

TRIBAL RUGS OF KURDISTAN *(Kurds)*

KNOT:	*Turkish*
WARP:	*wool or cotton*
WEFT:	*wool, double*
PILE:	*medium long, good-quality wool*
FRINGE:	*knotted at both ends*
SELVEDGE:	*several warp threads overcast with brown wool*

Kurdistan lies in what is now northwestern Iran, northern Iraq, southeastern Turkey, and the extreme northern tip of Syria. Kurdish tribes are not restricted to the loose boundaries of the Kurdistan region, but are widely scattered throughout western Iran and parts of Iraq, Turkey, and the Russian Caucasus (see Figure 13). Kurdish tribes are urbanized as well as nomadic or seminomadic. Rugs made by the nomadic and seminomadic tribes are referred to as Kurdish tribal rugs and are classed differently from the urban Kurdish tribes of Bijar and Senna.

Because characteristics of Kurdish tribal rugs vary according to the location of each tribe, individual rugs are often hard to identify. A strong Caucasian influence is evident among the northern Kurds; Anatolian elements are noticeable in the rugs of the western tribes. As a further complication in identification, the rugs may have a cotton warp and weft, a wool warp and weft, or a cotton warp and a wool weft. The pile is a heavy, good-quality wool. The weavers of the Jaffi tribe have a unique way of knotting their rugs, staggering knots so that they tie on the same pair of warp threads only in every second row of knots.*

The Herati, Mina Khani, and the Boteh are common designs used by the Kurdish tribes; however, designs vary among the tribes as often as do the weaving characteristics. (See Plate 30.)

---

* Murray Eiland, *Oriental Rugs: A Comprehensive Guide* (Greenwich, Conn.: New York Graphic Society, Ltd., 1973), p. 49.

SENNA *(Sehna, Senna, Sena)*

KNOT:	*Turkish*
WARP:	*cotton*
WEFT:	*cotton, single*
PILE:	*cut short*
FRINGE:	*plain or knotted at both ends*
SELVEDGE:	*several warp threads overcast with wool*

For several hundred years some of the finest Persian rugs have been woven in Senna (officially known as Sanandaj). The designs have changed very little over the years; the Herati pattern with a diamond-shaped medallion and the Boteh design are most often used. A repeated flower design (Gul-i-Mirza Ali or Guli Frank) indicates a definite French influence. (See Plate 31.)

Senna is the capital of the Iranian province of Kurdistan, a mountainous region in western Iran. The majority of the inhabitants of Senna, as well as most of the weavers, are Kurds of the Gurani tribe. These Kurds weave the closely knotted Senna rug only in the city; in the surrounding villages they weave the loosely knotted Kurdish tribal rugs.

The rugs of Senna are finely woven with good-quality wool. The warp in older rugs is often silk, in contrast to the cotton warp found in newer rugs. The Turkish knot is the only kind used in Senna rugs.

One of the finest kelims is woven in Senna and the surrounding area. (See Chapter 9.)

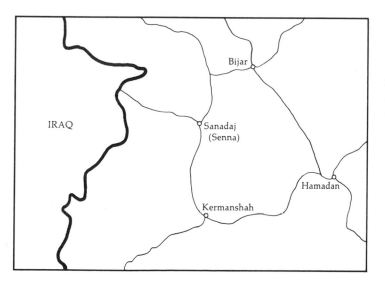

FIGURE 13:
*KURDISTAN
REGION*

opposite,
PLATE 30: *KURD*
4 ft. by 6 ft.

PLATE 32: *BIJAR*
2 ft. 2 in. by 3 ft.

BIJAR

KNOT:	*Turkish*
WARP:	*cotton (wool in older rugs)*
WEFT:	*cotton, wool, or both, triple*
PILE:	*cut short*
FRINGE:	kelim *at one end with knotted fringe at the other*
SELVEDGE:	*several warp threads overcast with wool*

The small town of Bijar is about forty miles northeast of Senna. The Bijar rugs are woven not only in Bijar, but also in a multitude of surrounding small villages.

Bijars are thick, tightly woven rugs with alternating warps depressed into the body of the rug. A unique feature of the wefts are the two thin cotton or wool wefts on either side of a thick wool weft thread. In weaving, the wefts are beaten down so firmly with a special comb used only in Bijar that the rug is quite stiff. The compactness of the fabric makes the carpet very sturdy.

The Herati pattern (with or without rectilinear medallion), Shah Abbas, and the Harshang (crab) designs are often used in the Bijar rugs in beautiful shades of dark blue, cherry red, and green (see Plates 32 and 33). Particularly intriguing is the Bijar sampler, in which various designs are illustrated by their incorporation into a single rug. In this way the weaving skills, as well as the individual designs, are passed on to future generations.

PLATE 33:
BIJAR SAMPLER
4 ft. by 6 ft.
Courtesy of Mr. and
Mrs. Tom Vance

HAMADAN

KNOT: *Turkish*
WARP: *cotton*
WEFT: *cotton, single*
PILE: *medium, good-quality wool*
FRINGE: kelim *at one end with plain fringe at the other*
SELVEDGE: *double overcast with wool*

Of all the rug-weaving centers in Iran, the Hamadan area is the largest in area as well as volume of rugs produced. The area is made up of hundreds of small towns and villages within a fifty-mile radius of the city of Hamadan (see Figure 14). The rugs of the more important of these small towns are marketed under their own name (*i.e.,* Bibikabad, Ingeles, and Dergazine). Since most of the rugs from the smaller, less important villages are marketed in the city of Hamadan, they are labeled as Hamadans, even though rugs made by each village possess their own identifiable characteristics.

The designs used in the Hamadan rugs are generally rectilinear; rod medallions and the Herati pattern are most often used (see Plates 34 and 35). During the 1920s and 1930s, many Hamadans were washed and painted. The weave varies from coarse to medium, the older Hamadans having a tighter weave. Excellent-quality wool is used, which makes the rugs wear exceptionally well.

Many Hamadans are available, both new and semi-antique. Although virtually all sizes are woven, the small sizes (3 by 5 to 4 by 6 feet) are most common.

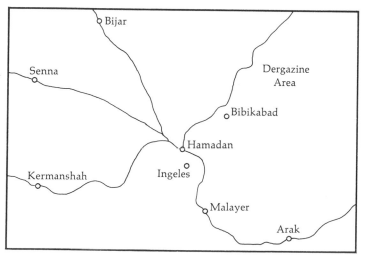

FIGURE 14:
HAMADAN AREA

PLATE 34: *HAMADAN (Semi-Antique) 3 ft. 4 in. by 5 ft. 3 in. Courtesy of Mr. and Mrs. Russell Summers*

PLATE 35: *HAMADAN, 3 ft. 4 in. by 4 ft. 11 in. Courtesy of Mr. Russell Herbert*

DERGAZINE *(Dergezine, Dargazin)*

KNOT: *Turkish*

WARP: *cotton*

WEFT: *cotton, single*

PILE: *medium, excellent-quality wool*

FRINGE: kelim *at one end with knotted fringe at the other*

SELVEDGE: *double overcast with wool*

If for no other reason, Dergazine is important for the volume of rugs produced over the years. The wealthiest district of the Hamadan area, the artisans of Dergazine have been weaving rugs for over four hundred years.* Some sixty small villages make up the Dergazine district, which is fifty miles northeast of Hamadan.

All Dergazines are similar in design, and have been strongly influenced by the Sarouk; both use a field filled with detached floral sprays. The ground colors are either red or navy blue. (See Plates 36 and 37.) During the 1920s and 1930s Dergazines, like the Sarouks, were washed and painted. The majority of Dergazine rugs are runners, although small rugs and mats are also woven. These rugs are extremely durable.

---

* A. Cecil Edwards, *The Persian Carpet* (London: Duckworth, 1975), p. 91.

PLATE 36: *DERGAZINE*
3 ft. 6 in. by 5 ft. 2 in.
Courtesy of Mr. and Mrs. Richard LeNoir

opposite,
PLATE 37: *DERGAZINE*
3 ft. 4 in. by 5 ft. 2 in.
Courtesy of Mr. and
Mrs. Paul Roberts

INGELES *(Ingelas, Injilas, Angelas)*

KNOT:	*Turkish*
WARP:	*cotton*
WEFT:	*cotton, single*
PILE:	*medium to medium long, excellent-quality wool*
FRINGE:	kelim *at one end with plain fringe at the other*
SELVEDGE:	*double overcast with wool*

Ingeles, a small village south of Hamadan, produces one of the best-quality rugs made in the Hamadan district. Only two designs are used, the Herati and the Mir-i-boteh. These can be woven either with or without a center medallion. The ground color is a cherry red with borders of navy and white. (See Plate 38.) Most of the rug production of Ingeles is in small sizes (3 by 5 to 4 by 6 feet) or runners.

BIBIKABAD

KNOT:	*Turkish*
WARP:	*cotton*
WEFT:	*cotton, single, occasionally dyed blue*
PILE:	*medium long, heavy, good-quality wool*
FRINGE:	*plain fringe at both ends*
SELVEDGE:	*overcast with wool*

The rugs labeled as Bibikabad are made in the small villages of Bibikabad and Ainabad, which lie approximately thirty miles northeast of Hamadan. The Herati and the Mir-i-boteh are the only designs woven, and appear either with or without a center medallion. The colors are navy blue, madder red, and ivory. (See Plate 39.) Bibikabads are woven in larger sizes (9 by 12 to 10 by 17 feet); smaller rugs are uncommon. These carpets are loosely woven with good-quality wool, making them ideal for heavy traffic areas. The *jufti*, or false knot (see page 22), has appeared in recent rugs, so caution should be used when buying them.

PLATE 39: *BIBIKABAD*
4 ft. 2 in. by 4 ft. 8 in.
Courtesy of
Mr. and Mrs. Jack Florin

SAROUK AND THE ARAK WEAVING AREA *(Saruk)*

KNOT:	*Persian*
WARP:	*cotton*
WEFT:	*cotton, double, usually dyed blue*
PILE:	*short, good-quality wool, tightly woven*
FRINGE:	*kelim at one end with knotted fringe at the other, or knotted fringe at both ends*
SELVEDGE:	*double overcast with wool the same color as the ground*

Sarouk rugs are woven not only in Sarouk but in Arak and many of the small surrounding-area villages (see Figure 15). Thousands of Sarouks were imported to the United States from the turn of the century until 1960, at which time they were diverted to fill the surging demand of the European market. The Sarouks that were made for the U.S. market varied little in design, having a floral field filled with detached floral sprays and a central floral-bouquet motif. The ground color was rose red to maroon, and nearly all the rugs were washed and painted. The main border was a navy blue Herati border pattern. These tightly woven rugs were made in all sizes from the smallest mats to large gallery sizes (1 by 2 to 15 by 30 feet).

The newer Sarouks, most of which find their way to the European market, have a medallion-and-corner design or use the Shah Abbas pattern. Ivory is often used as a ground color.

FIGURE 15: *ARAK WEAVING AREA*

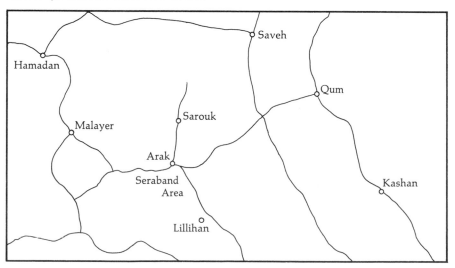

Other rugs from the same area are woven with the detached floral spray "Sarouk" pattern. (See Plate 40.) The difference between these rugs and the Sarouks is the tightness of weave. While these rugs may be identical to the Sarouk in pattern, they are not Sarouks; in order of decreasing quality they are labeled Arak, Sultanabad, Mahal, and Mushkabad. The latter two are inferior bazaar-quality carpets often woven with "skin" or dead wool and inferior dyes.

PLATE 40: *SAROUK*
3 ft. 3 in. by 5 ft. 2 in.
Courtesy of Mr. and
Mrs. Donald Dieterich

ARAK / SULTANABAD

KNOT: *Persian*
WARP: *cotton*
WEFT: *cotton, double, dyed blue*
PILE: *medium to medium long, good-quality wool*
FRINGE: kelim *at one end with knotted fringe at the other, or knotted fringe at both ends*
SELVEDGE: *double overcast with wool the same color as the ground*

Arak and Sultanabad rugs are woven in the west-central Iranian town of Arak (once called Sultanabad) as well as in the surrounding area. Though rugs labeled as Araks and Sultanabads are made in the same town or area, they are different rugs, although the variation is only in tightness of weave. As mentioned in the section under Sarouk, the Arak is a slightly higher quality rug than the Sultanabad. These generalizations also apply to the non-Sarouk patterns woven in the Arak area. The Herati, Shah Abbas, and the medallion designs are all used frequently in and around Arak. Common ground colors are red, blue, and ivory. The larger sizes are more often woven, especially in the 8 by 10 to 9 by 12 feet sizes. Though these rugs are not as tightly woven as Sarouks, they are made with good-quality wool and wear extremely well.

LILLIHAN *(Lilihan)*

KNOT: *Persian*
WARP: *cotton*
WEFT: *cotton, single*
PILE: *medium short*
FRINGE: kelim *at one end with plain fringe at the other*
SELVEDGE: *double overcast with blue wool*

Twenty-five miles south of Arak lies the small town of Lillihan. Rugs were produced here that were very similar to the Sarouk in design, but resemble the Hamadan in weave. Lillihans are easily recognized by their rose-pink or rose-red ground, and by the blue and azure colors used in the motifs and borders. The typical design is an overall floral pattern in which floral sprays surround a central floral-bouquet medallion. (See Plates 41 and 42.) As with the Sarouks of the 1920s and 1930s, most of the Lillihans were chemically washed and then painted.

Very few Lillihans are being woven today; most of the town's weaving has been diverted to producing Sarouks. Many semi-antique Lillihans may be found, however, especially in the smaller (3 by 5 to 4 by 6 feet) sizes.

PLATE 41: *LILLIIIAN (Antique), 4 ft. by 7 ft. Courtesy of Mr. and Mrs. Clair Harrah*

SERABAND

KNOT: *Turkish, occasionally Persian*

WARP: *cotton*

WEFT: *cotton, often dyed blue; double*

PILE: *medium, thick heavy wool*

FRINGE: *kelim at one end with plain or knotted fringe at the other*

SELVEDGE: *double overcast with wool*

Seraband rugs are made in the Sarawan district, about twenty miles southwest of Arak. Despite the proximity to Arak, Seraband rugs are far more closely related to the rugs of Hamadan. Rugs have been woven in this area for several hundred years.

The antique Seraband, called the Mir-Seraband, is a quite different rug from those produced in the area today. Since they have not been woven since the turn of the century, Mir-Serabands are rare today. With a tighter weave and of much finer quality than its loosely woven present-day counterpart, Mir-Serabands were usually woven in the Mir-i-boteh pattern, although the Herati design was occasionally used. The present-day Seraband always has the Mir-i-boteh design, and the main border continues to be ivory with the *Schekeri* design (a continuous vine with *boteh*). The ground color is either red or dark blue. (See Plate 43.) The Mir-Serabands were woven in small sizes or *kelleis* (5 by 15 feet); the modern Serabands are found in sizes ranging from small to 8 by 10 feet.

Not all Mir-i-boteh rugs are Serabands. The Arak area weaves a tightly knotted rug called the Seraband-Sarouk; these excellent-quality rugs resemble the Sarouk in weave and usually come in 4 by 6 to 9 by 12 feet sizes.

opposite,
PLATE 42: *LILLIHAN,*
3 ft. 3 in. by 4 ft. 6 in.

opposite,
PLATE 43: *SERABAND (Portion)*
7 ft. by 10 ft.
Courtesy of Mr. and
Mrs. Porter Godard

PLATE 44: *MALAYER (Hamadan)*
2 ft. by 3 ft.
Courtesy of Mr. and
Mrs. George Sinkinson

MALAYER

KNOT:	*Turkish, Persian*
WARP:	*cotton*
WEFT:	*cotton; single or double*
PILE:	*medium*
FRINGE:	kelim *at one end with knotted fringe at the other*
SELVEDGE:	*double overcast with blue wool*

Halfway between Hamadan and Arak are the approximately 120 villages of the Malayer district that surround the town of Malayer. The villages northwest of Malayer, toward Hamadan, produce a carpet very similar to the Hamadan in weave. (See Plate 44.) The villages southeast of Malayer, toward Arak, weave a fine-quality carpet very similar in weave to the Sarouk. Commonly called Malayer Sarouks, these rugs are Turkish-knotted, a feature that at times provides the only clue in distinguishing them from a Sarouk. Rugs produced in Josan, the most important of these minor villages, are known on the rug market as Josan Sarouks.

FERAHAN

KNOT: *Persian*
WARP: *cotton*
WEFT: *cotton, double*
PILE: *short, finely knotted*
FRINGE: kelim *at one end with knotted fringe at the other*
SELVEDGE: *overcast with wool*

The Ferahan district is located between Arak and Sarouk. Few, if any, Ferahan carpets have been made since the turn of the century. The weaving in this area is now limited to Sarouks, Araks, and the lower quality rugs of the Arak area.

The Herati pattern, with or without a medallion, was the most common design woven, although the Mina Khani and the Guli Henna were also used. Ferahans featured either a dark blue or red ground, with green often used in the motifs and the main border (see Plate 45). Most Ferahans were woven in small sizes. They have become difficult to obtain in recent times.

PLATE 45: *FERAHAN*
3 ft. by 5 ft. Courtesy of
Mr. John Campbell, Jr.

VERAMIN

KNOT: *Persian*
WARP: *cotton*
WEFT: *cotton; single or double*
PILE: *medium short, excellent-quality wool*
FRINGE: *small* kelim *with knotted fringe*
SELVEDGE: *overcast with wool*

Approximately thirty miles south of Tehran is the central Iranian town of Veramin. A rug which is called a Veramin may be woven either in Veramin or in one of its surrounding villages.

There are two designs most commonly found in Veramin carpets. These are the Mina Khani and the Zil-i-soltan.

In the Mina Khani design, four flower motifs or rosettes are connected by vines, all of which surround a palmette and four smaller palmette motifs. The floral motifs are usually some combination of shades of rust-red, yellow, or ivory. Typical of the Mina Khani-design Veramin is a blue field.

The Zil-i-soltan design is also called the "vase-of-roses" design. It is not as common in Veramin carpets as the Mina Khani design. The Zil-i-soltan motifs are relatively large in comparison with the area of the field. An ivory or red ground is used with this type of design.

Veramins are tightly knotted on a cotton foundation; the wool used for the pile is of excellent quality. The tightness of weave and quality of wool yield a very durable carpet. Many Veramins are given a chemical wash to soften and mellow their appearance, even though their unwashed colors are not harsh. Veramins are generally small, ranging in size up to 6 by 9 feet (approximately 2 by 3 meters).

PLATE 46: *VERAMIN (Mina Khani Design) 3 ft. 7 in. by 4 ft. 9 in. Courtesy of Mrs. Russell Summers*

71

ISFAHAN *(Ispahan, Esfahan)*

KNOT: *Persian*
WARP: *cotton or silk*
WEFT: *cotton, double*
PILE: *short, good- to excellent-grade wool*
FRINGE: *narrow* kelim *with plain fringe at both ends*
SELVEDGE: *double overcast with wool*

Isfahan is regarded as one of the most beautiful cities in the world. Carpet-weaving here can be traced back to the sixteenth century, when Isfahan was the capital of Persia under Shah Abbas. The weaving looms were destroyed in the Afghan invasion of 1722, and little weaving was done until the carpet industry had its rebirth in the early 1920s. Most of these carpets were then exported to Europe. These rugs were woven with inferior wool; their colors were too bright and their pile too short, and they were not popular in Europe. After World War II, the quality greatly improved, and many of the rugs were produced for the home market.

Overall, the Isfahan is one of the finest rugs woven in Iran today. At its best the Isfahan is unsurpassed in quality.

The designs of Isfahan and Nain are very similar; the Shah Abbas and the medallion-and-corner (see Plate 47) are the two most commonly woven designs, although the Tree-of-life and prayer designs are also used in Isfahan. In the field, an ivory or pastel blue are the most frequently used colors; red grounds are also woven.

Isfahans have never been imported in great quantities to the U.S. market. Although a variety of sizes are available, the most common sizes found are 4 by 7 to 8 by 10 feet.

opposite,
PLATE 47: *ISFAHAN, 4 ft. by 6 ft.*
Courtesy of Mr. and Mrs. F.A. Brubaker

PLATE 48: *NAIN, 3 ft. by 5 ft. Courtesy of Mr. and Mrs. William Campbell, Jr.*

NAIN

KNOT: *Persian*
WARP: *cotton or silk*
WEFT: *cotton or silk, double*
PILE: *short, excellent-quality wool*
FRINGE: *knotted at both ends*
SELVEDGE: *double overcast with wool*

Sixty miles east of Isfahan lies the small town of Nain, the carpet-makers of which produce one of the finest carpets in Iran. Nain artisans began weaving rugs only in the early 1930s, after having been renowned for centuries for the fine woolen cloth made there. When the import of western fabrics and fashions brought about the decline of the cloth-weaving industry, craftsmen undertook the weaving of carpets in the same tradition of excellence. Their weave is comparable in knot count to the best of the antique carpets.

Nain designs are very similar to those of Isfahan. The Shah Abbas (with an ivory ground) and the medallion designs (with blue or, more rarely, red ground) are woven most often (see Plate 48). Silk may be used in the Nain to outline many of the motifs; all-silk rugs are also made. Measured against the total volume of rugs made in Nain, very few Nains are exported to the United States. The rugs are quite expensive, and those that are imported are usually in the smaller sizes (4 by 6 feet or smaller).

However fine the knot count, Nain rugs lack variety in the designs and colors used.

QUM *(Ghoum, Qom)*

KNOT:	*Persian*
WARP:	*cotton or silk*
WEFT:	*cotton or silk*
PILE:	*short, excellent-quality wool*
FRINGE:	*knotted at both ends*
SELVEDGE:	*double overcast with wool*

Qum, ninety miles south of Tehran, is one of the holiest cities in Iran; Mohammed's daughter Fatima is buried here. The weaving industry of Qum was begun in the early 1930s by merchants from Kashan.

A wide variety of designs are used in Qum: the Panel design, Garden design, Zil-i-soltan (vase of roses), Boteh, prayer, and Shah Abbas. All are beautifully and skillfully executed, with a wide array of colors used in the motifs and grounds (see Plates 49 and 50). Not only are beautiful all-silk rugs woven, but silk is often woven into wool rugs to outline and accent the motifs. A Qum is regarded as one of the finest rugs made today and, as one might expect, its quality is reflected in its price. Small sizes are most common.

PLATE 49: *QUM (Garden Design)*
3 ft. 2 in. by 5 ft.
Courtesy of Mr. and
Mrs. Russell Summers

opposite,
PLATE 50: *QUM (Prayer Design)*
3 ft. 5 in. by 5 ft. 8 in.

PLATE 51: *KASHAN (Prayer Design)*
3 ft. 8 in. by 5 ft. 2 in.
Courtesy of Dr. and Mrs. John Campbell

KASHAN

KNOT: *Persian*
WARP: *cotton*
WEFT: *cotton, double*
PILE: *short, excellent quality*
FRINGE: *knotted at both ends*
SELVEDGE: *double overcast with wool*

Kashan is located in central Iran about 150 miles south of Tehran. The carpet-weaving industry of Kashan, like that of Isfahan, was destroyed when the Afghans invaded Persia in 1722. Since weaving was begun again in the late nineteenth century, Kashan has established and maintained a reputation for making one of the finest Persian rugs.

The traditional designs woven in Kashan are the Shah Abbas and the medallion-and-corner, with a red ground. More recently, Kashan has adopted the Garden design with an ivory ground, although the traditional designs are still woven. Kashan is noted also for its prayer rugs, which artisans weave in either wool or silk (see Plate 51).

JOSHAGHAN

KNOT:	*Persian*
WARP:	*cotton*
WEFT:	*cotton, double usually dyed blue*
PILE:	*short to medium, heavy, good-quality wool*
FRINGE:	*small* kelim *with plain fringe at both ends*
SELVEDGE:	*double overcast with blue wool*

Rugs have been woven in the central Iranian village of Joshaghan for several hundred years. Designs have changed very little, and are restricted to a few variations of the medallion-and-corner pattern. Separate Guli Henna, Mina Khani, and Bid Majnūm (Weeping Willow) motifs are clustered in diamond shapes scattered throughout the field, and a diamond-shaped medallion, often outlined in white, is sometimes present. The ground color is usually madder red, with blue and white used in the motifs. (See Plate 52.)

The wool comes from the sheep of surrounding mountain area and is of excellent quality.

PLATE 52: *JOSHAGHAN*
3 ft. 6 in. by 5 ft. 4 in.

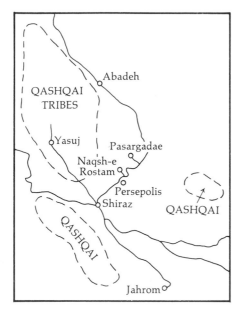

FIGURE 16:
FARS DISTRICT

PLATE 53: *SHIRAZ*
4 ft. by 6 ft.

SHIRAZ

KNOT:	*Persian*
WARP:	*wool; dark brown or natural, or a mixture of both*
WEFT:	*wool; double; dark brown, natural or dyed red*
PILE:	*medium to medium long*
FRINGE:	*wide* kelim *(often striped) with plain fringe*
SELVEDGE:	*overcast with alternating colored wool*

Rugs that are commonly called Shiraz are woven by many different nomadic and seminomadic tribes of the Fars region (see Figure 16). These rugs derive their name from the fact that they are marketed in Shiraz, the provincial capital.

Small Persian villages scattered around Shiraz and a loosely organized federation of many unrelated Arab, Turkish, and Luri tribes are the largest and most important sources of rugs in the province—about 80 percent of the province's total rug output. Each of the villages produces rugs generally indistinguishable in quality and design from those of the other villages and are grouped and labeled as Shiraz, rather than by their tribal or village origin. These village-area rugs usually have a Persian knot and a single woolen weft thread. The rugs woven by the federation may either be made with a Persian or a Turkish knot or a double or a single-weft thread, depending on the individual tribe.

The differences between the rugs of the Persian Villagers and those of the recently settled nomadic tribes are often hazy. There is often inter-marriage between the villagers and the nomads of the same plain or valley. It is quite difficult in such cases to determine the origin of a rug from that area.

The rugs of Shiraz have geometric designs; a rectilinear pole medallion, as well as many other geometric designs, are used. The selvedges in the older Shiraz rugs have a barber-pole effect, with two or more alternating bands of colors; however, the barber-pole effect may not always be found in newer rugs. (See Plates 53 through 55.)

PLATE 54: *SHIRAZ, (Antique) 3 ft. by 5 ft.*

PLATE 55: *SHIRAZ, 3 ft. 6 in. by 5 ft. 3 in. Courtesy of Mr. and Mrs. Richard LeNoir*

QASHQAI *(Kashgai, Ghasqai)*

KNOT:	*Turkish*
WARP:	*wool*
WEFT:	*wool, double*
PILE:	*medium, thick, excellent-quality wool*
FRINGE:	kelim *with plain or knotted fringe at both ends*
SELVEDGE:	*overcast with alternating colors of wool*

The Qashqai are the best weavers and the most prosperous of all of the tribes of Fars. Women do all of the weaving and take great pride in their rugs. The wool, which comes from Qashqai sheep, is washed, spun, and dyed with great care. It is soft and develops a beautiful patina.

Designs are typically geometric, consisting of a Tree-of-life or a diamond-shaped medallion or medallions. Small stylized figures and other small geometric motifs are scattered throughout the field. (See Plate 56.)

Most of the Qashqai weaving is in small rugs, saddle bags, or tent bags. The excellence of the Qashqai rugs is reflected in their price; they are more expensive than most nomadic or seminomadic rugs.

PLATE 56: *QASHQAI, 3 ft. by 5 ft.*
Courtesy of Dr. and Mrs. L.A. Graham

82

PLATE 57: *YELEMEH*
3 ft. 5 in. by 5 ft. 2 in.

YELEMEH

KNOT:	*Persian or Turkish*
WARP:	*wool*
WEFT:	*dark-brown wool; single or double*
PILE:	*medium, soft, good-quality wool*
FRINGE:	*knotted at both ends*
SELVEDGE:	*two colors alternating in diagonal stripes*

Yelemeh rugs are relatively new to the western market, having been made only since World War II. These rugs are produced by both the Persian Villagers and the Qashqai in the area between Shiraz and Abadeh. They are rectilinear in design, with latch-hooked diamond-shaped medallions; small geometric motifs are found throughout the field. The newer rugs have beautiful shades of green, yellow, orange, red, and blue, whereas the older rugs have more red, blue, and beige (see Plate 57).

The Yelemehs may be woven with the Persian or Turkish knot, depending on whether they are made by the Persian Villagers or the Qashqai. The warp and weft are usually wool, with a dark brown weft thread, although in the village rugs cotton may be used. The pile is a soft, good-quality wool.

ABADEH

KNOT: *Persian*

WARP: *cotton*

WEFT: *cotton, dyed light blue, double*

PILE: *short, good-quality wool*

FRINGE: *narrow* kelim *with either plain or knotted fringe at both ends*

SELVEDGE: *double overcast with wool*

Abadeh, located approximately halfway between Isfahan and Shiraz, has been producing carpets for export for only the past thirty years. Most of the designs woven have been borrowed from other weaving areas. The diamond medallion pattern with corner rosettes (see Plate 58) is an adaptation of a Qashqai tribal pattern. The Zil-i-soltan, or vase of roses, design is also a common design woven in Abadeh.

The rugs of Abadeh are woven with good-quality wool and are recommended for their durability. The most common colors found in the Abadehs are red, cream, and blue.

PLATE 58: *ABADEH, 2 ft. 4 in. by 3 ft. 7 in. Courtesy of Mr. and Mrs. David Elias*

84

KERMAN

KNOT:	*Persian*
WARP:	*cotton*
WEFT:	*cotton, double*
PILE:	*medium length*
FRINGE:	*knotted fringe at both ends*
SELVEDGE:	*overcast with wool the same color as the ground*

The province of Kerman is an area in southeastern Iran; the city of Kerman is its provincial capital and main city. Kerman rugs are woven in the city as well as in many of the surrounding villages. Weaving in Kerman can be traced as far back as the seventeenth century, although the rug industry remained small scale until its overall expansion in the late nineteenth century.

The Kerman rugs have always been favorites on the western market. All Kermans are floral, but variations are made to suit the tastes of the three major markets of the United States, Europe, and Iran. The American Kerman is known for its pastel colors, central medallion, and either an open or a semi-open field (see Plate 59). The Iranian Kerman has a cochineal-red ground with a central medallion and an open field; it has a tighter weave and shorter pile than those imported to the United States. The European Kerman has small detached floral sprays with a central medallion and comes in pastel colors (see Plate 60). All sizes are woven, from the smallest mats to large gallery sizes.

LAVER KERMAN

Some of the finest antique Kerman rugs came from the small village of Ravar, which in the West is known as Laver. Today the rug-makers of Ravar weave Kermans indistinguishable from those made in the city of Kerman proper.

KERMANSHAH

The labeling of rugs as "Kermanshah" is controversial, since few disputed rugs were ever woven there. The town of Kermanshah is a Kurd tribal village 900 miles from Kerman, noted for its wool marketplace. Any rugs woven there are Kurds, and bear the definite characteristics of Kurdish rather than Kerman rugs.

The designation "Kermanshah" might lead one to believe that a rug bearing that name is a superior Kerman or Kerman-design rug. "Kermanshah" has been generally accepted as referring to design rather than origin, specifically, an intricate all-over floral pattern, either with or without a central medallion. No new rug should be referred to as a Kermanshah; if it was woven in the town of Kermanshah, it is a Kurd; if it displays Kerman characteristics, it is a Kerman.

PLATE 59:
KERMAN
(American Design)
5 ft. 2 in.
by 8 ft. 4 in.
Courtesy of
Mr. and Mrs.
Raymond Allen

PLATE 60: *KERMAN (European Design) 5 ft. 11 in. by 8 ft. 11 in.*
Courtesy of Mrs. Russell Summers

PLATE 61: *AFSHAR (Morgi Design) signed Reza Khan*
2 ft. by 1 ft. Courtesy of Mr. and Mrs. John Griffis

AFSHAR

KNOT:	*Persian or Turkish*
WARP:	*cotton or wool*
WEFT:	*single cotton, double wool*
PILE:	*medium, very good–quality wool*
FRINGE:	*knotted or plain fringe at both ends*
SELVEDGE:	*double overcast with blue wool*

Afshari rugs are made by nomads and villagers whose life-styles are very similar to those of the Qashqai and Persian Villagers of Fars. The Afshari area is to the south and southwest of the city of Kerman.

Afshari villagers weave their rugs with a Persian knot on a cotton foundation, while the nomads use a Turkish knot on a woolen foundation. The Afshari employ a variety of designs: large floral sprays borrowed from Kerman, repeated rows of large geometric *boteh*, diamond-shaped medallions similar to those of Shiraz, and the *Morgi* design. The Morgi ("hen") pattern (see Plate 61) is an imaginative design that originated with the Afshari, although it has since been adopted in the Fars region. A geometric motif, resembling a chicken, is repeated throughout the field. Afshari rugs are usually small, rarely over 5 by 7 feet. Vegetable dyes are still used; red, cream, and blue are common ground colors.

YEZD

KNOT: *Persian*
WARP: *cotton*
WEFT: *cotton, double, dyed blue*
PILE: *medium in length*
FRINGE: *narrow* kelim *at both ends with fringe*
SELVEDGE: *overcast with blue wool*

Carpets were woven in Yezd as early as the seventeenth century, but until recently the weaving was on a very small scale. Few of the Yezd carpets have been imported to the United States, although they are quite popular on the European and the Persian markets.

The Herati pattern and the medallion-and-corner design appear most often in Yezd rugs. The older Yezd carpets resemble the Tabriz in structure; the newer carpets are more similar to the Kermans. Usually large and room-size, these carpets are very durable. Red and blue are the most common ground colors, but bright colors such as yellows and creams are also found in the designs.

CARPETS OF KHURASAN *(Khurassan)*

Occupying most of the northeast quadrant of Iran is the huge province of Khurasan (see Figure 17). Northern Khurasan is one of the major wool-producing areas of Iran. Rugs from the Khurasan province fall into three major classifications: Khurasan, Mashad, and Birjand.

MASHAD

KNOT: *Persian*
WARP: *cotton, knots tied on four warp threads*
WEFT: *cotton*
PILE: *medium, good-quality wool*
FRINGE: *plain fringe at both ends*
SELVEDGE: *double overcast with wool*

Rugs that originate in the Mashad area need to be divided into two groups: the *Mashad* rugs, woven in the small towns and villages surrounding the town of Mashad, and the *Turkibaff*, which are woven in the city of Mashad proper.

The two kinds of rugs are similar in design; the Shah Abbas design, with or without a medallion, may be used with a dark cochineal-red field. The other common design is the Herati with medallion and corners, generally woven in several shades of blue and ivory. Both groups of rugs are usually woven in large, room sizes, 9 by 12 feet, or larger.

The Mashads are tied with a Persian knot on four warp threads instead of the usual two. Because this has always been the case with Mashad rugs and is an accepted standard *in these rugs only*, they are not termed *jufti*. The pile is a soft, thick wool obtained from the fall shearing, which does not wear as well as that taken in the spring shearing. (See Plate 62.)

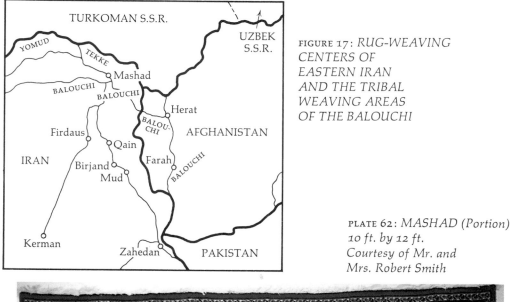

FIGURE 17: *RUG-WEAVING CENTERS OF EASTERN IRAN AND THE TRIBAL WEAVING AREAS OF THE BALOUCHI*

PLATE 62: *MASHAD (Portion) 10 ft. by 12 ft. Courtesy of Mr. and Mrs. Robert Smith*

TURKIBAFF

KNOT: *Turkish*
WARP: *cotton, knots tied on two warp threads*
WEFT: *cotton*
PILE: *medium, excellent-quality wool*
FRINGE: *plain fringe at both ends*
SELVEDGE: *double overcast with wool*

The Turkibaff carpets are woven with the Turkish knot on two warp threads. These rugs are a better quality than Mashads, and are generally woven with wool taken in the spring shearing.

KHURASAN

No new carpets are being imported as Khurasans. Most authorities use the term to denote antique and semi-antique rugs with a Herati pattern, from the Khurasan province. These had a unique weft structure in which a single weft was passed between three or four rows of knots; then, three or four wefts were passed between the next two rows of knots, giving the back of the carpet a ribbed appearance. These rugs are extremely rare today.

MUD (Moute)

Another excellent quality rug of the Khurasan area is woven in the small village of Mud. The Mud is usually woven with a Herati pattern on an ivory ground. (See Plate 63.)

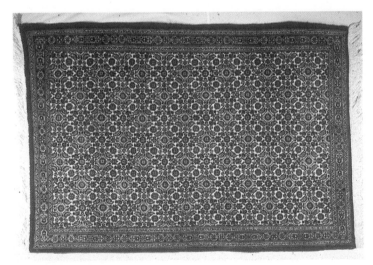

PLATE 63: *MUD, 3 ft. 5 in. by 5 ft. 2 in. Courtesy of Mr. and Mrs. Roger Wilkerson*

BIRJAND

The rugs labeled as Birjands now refer to the lowest grades of carpet woven in the Khurasan province. Comparable in quality to the Mahal rugs of the Arak area, Birjands are woven in the town of Birjand and in the surrounding area. The same designs used in Mashad are woven in Birjand, as is the practice of tying Persian knots around four warp threads.

BALOUCHI *(Baluchi, Belouchi)*

KNOT:	*Persian*
WARP:	*wool or cotton (new rugs from Iran)*
WEFT:	*wool, usually dark colored*
PILE:	*short to medium (new rugs from Iran)*
FRINGE:	*wide* kelim *often decorated with small motifs or stripes*
SELVEDGE:	*double selvedge overcast with dark-colored goat's hair*

Contrary to what might be expected, Balouchi rugs are *not* woven in Balouchistan. They are made in the Khurasan province of northeast Iran, and in the west and southwest portion of Afghanistan, by Balouchi tribes and also by a few Arab tribes near Firdaus. In Iran the rugs woven by the Balouchi tribes are marketed in Mashad; those woven in Afghanistan are usually marketed in Herat.

Balouchi rugs resemble Turkoman rugs not only in color but also in some designs, which may vary depending on the rug's origin. The Arab tribes around Firdaus weave a rug which may employ either diagonal or vertical stripes. Turkoman-style (Tekke) *guls* may be woven by Balouchis living in northern areas near Turkoman tribes. Balouchi tribes are noted

PLATE 64: *BALOUCHI (Boteh Design) Woven in Iran, 3 ft. by 5 ft. Courtesy of Mr. and Mrs. Richard LeNoir*

PLATE 65: *BALOUCHI (Prayer Design)*
Woven in Afghanistan, 3 ft. by 5 ft.
Courtesy of Mr. and Mrs. Paul Roberts

PLATE 66: *BALOUCHI (Semi-Antique)*
Woven in Iran, 3 ft. by 5 ft.
Courtesy of Dr. Theodore Herbert

for their weaving of prayer rugs. Many different motifs may fill the *mihrab*, but the stylized Tree-of-life design is most commonly used. The running-dog or Greek key border is a common characteristic of most Balouchi rugs. (See Plates 64 and 66.)

As with Turkoman rugs and those made by the nomadic tribes of Iran, Balouchi rugs are woven on a horizontal loom. The warp thread may be either wool or cotton. The newer Balouchi rugs of Iran have a cotton warp and a thicker pile than those made in Afghanistan. The weft is usually single and made either of sheep's wool or a mixture of sheep's wool and goat's hair. The knot used is the Persian. The pile is of good-quality wool; camel's wool is used on rare occasions.

Semi-antique and antique Balouchi rugs often have at each end a wide *kelim*, which may be decorated with multicolored stripes or small motifs. Selvedges are double and made of black goat's hair. The colors of older rugs are more muted, with shades of dark red, brown, black, and camel; the newer rugs are somewhat brighter.

Both new and semi-antique Balouchi rugs are available. Most of these rugs are in small sizes (3 by 5 to 4 by 6 feet).

5

Caucasian Rugs

CAUCASIAN RUGS are a study all their own. Identifying a rug as Caucasian is not very difficult, since they have a woolen foundation, brilliant colors, and highly stylized, geometric motifs. Further classification as to town or region gets a little more complicated, as design and color are not always the clues to identification in Caucasian rugs as they are for the Persian rugs.

The Caucasus Mountains form a natural boundary between Europe and Asia, rising in the narrow strip of land between the Black and Caspian Seas. Writing in 1807, German anthropologist Johann Friederich Blumenbach stated that the inhabitants of the Caucasus Mountain region comprised the purest example of the "white" race, thereby deriving the term "Caucasian." It was also in the Caucasus Mountains that Zeus chained Prometheus for giving the fire of the gods to mortals.

Although the Caucasus has long been isolated from the rest of the world, there has been a great cultural interchange among the many ethnic

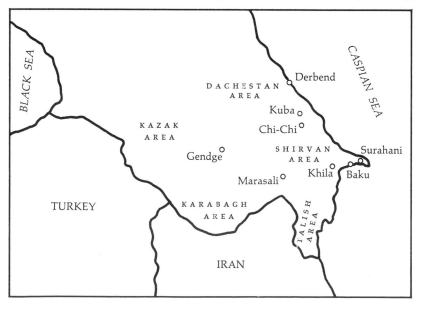

FIGURE 18:
*WEAVING
AREAS OF THE
CAUCASUS*

groups and tribes inhabiting the area (see Figure 18). The southeast area (Karabagh, Baku, and part of Shirvan) reflects the Persian influence; in the northwest area (Kazak) there is a strong Armenian, Kurd, and Azeri Turk influence. In the northeast (Daghestan and Kuba) most inhabitants are Moslem. These nomadic and seminomadic tribesmen and villagers affect and are affected by the other tribes with whom they meet during the course of their travels. Although each village or tribe weaves designs unique to its area, there is a great exchange or borrowing of designs between the peoples. The diagonal stripe, which is used most often in Gendge, will appear in Kazak or even in Daghestan, for example.

Dates were quite often woven into Caucasian rugs. Most of these dates were based on the Moslem calendar. See *Dates*, p. 34, for conversion procedure. Dates based on the Christian calendar were woven into rugs from the western Caucasus regions by Armenian Christians; western numerals generally were used.

Large quantities of Caucasian rugs were imported for both the European and American markets from the late 1800s until about 1935, when production for export ceased. After World War II, the Soviet government began to revitalize the carpet industry. By the early 1960s Caucasian rugs, especially Kazak designs, began to reappear on European markets.

KAZAK

KNOT:	*Turkish*
WARP:	*natural-colored wool, thick (three-ply)*
WEFT:	*wool usually dyed red, double*
PILE:	*long, thick, heavy wool (shaggy appearance)*
FRINGE:	*looped at one end; knotted at the other*
SELVEDGE:	*several warp threads overcast with wool that has usually been dyed red*

The Kazak area, composed of numerous small weaving districts, lies in the southwestern part of the Caucasus. This area was inhabited primarily by Azeri Turks (Azerbaijans), Armenians, and Kurds. These ethnic groups wove a substantial number of rugs, each with their own unique characteristics.

The rugs of Kazak are among the most easily identified of the Caucasian rugs. This is due to their bold geometric designs, brilliant colors, and unique structural characteristics. Many Kazak designs are large-scaled in comparison to the field, but other designs are relatively small and may be repeated in rows or columns in the field. Quite often, the field is dominated by a single medallion or by several medallions.

The foundation of Kazak carpets is composed of three-ply, natural-colored wool warp threads, with wool weft threads that often are dyed red. The wefts are usually double, although it is not unusual to find three or more. Kazaks were woven with a small *kelim* with looped fringe at one end. At the opposite end, the fringe is either knotted or plaited. (See Plate 69.) Kazaks were woven in small sizes, up to 6 by 9 feet (2 by 3 meters).

PLATE 67: *KAZAK*
(*Armenian*)
3 ft. 11 in. by 8 ft. 7 in.

PLATE 68: *KAŻAK, (Prayer Design),
2 ft. 10 in. by 5 ft. 2 in.*

PLATE 69: *Kazak, Kelim and Braided Fringe*

PLATE 70: *GENDGE, 3 ft. by 5 ft.*
Courtesy of Dr. and Mrs. L.A. Graham

GENDGE *(Gendje, Geunge)*

KNOT:	*Turkish*
WARP:	*wool*
WEFT:	*wool; three, four, or more*
PILE:	*medium long*
FRINGE:	*looped at one end; knotted at the other*
SELVEDGE:	*several warp threads overcast with wool*

For centuries Gendge has been a trade center because of its strategic location on caravan routes and, more recently, on the rail line. It is situated halfway between the Black Sea and the Caspian Sea.

Structurally, the Gendge rugs differ very little from those of Kazak; however, quality may vary greatly, depending on the area in which the rugs were woven. Colors tend to be paler and designs smaller scaled than those of Kazak. The design most commonly associated with the Gendge is one of diagonal stripes covering the entire field. Each stripe contains a small repeating motif, such as a *boteh.* (See Plate 70.)

KARABAGH

KNOT: *Turkish*
WARP: *brown wool (occasionally cotton)*
WEFT: *wool (occasionally cotton)*
PILE: *medium long*
FRINGE: *looped at one end; knotted at the other*
SELVEDGE: *two warp threads usually overcast with wool*

Like those of Gendje, the rugs of Karabagh are similar in structure to the Kazak, to the extent that it is sometimes hard to tell the difference. The Karabaghs tend to be more floral, more finely knotted, and to have shorter pile than the Kazaks. The Karabagh area is located east and south of the Kazak area in the southern part of the Caucasus along the Iranian border.

The Chelaberd ("sunburst" or Eagle Kazak) contains one or more radial medallions in the field (see Plate 71). A strong Persian influence is evident in some of the designs; curvilinear (a Savonnerie-type floral) as well as rectilinear (Herati and *boteh*) motifs are used. (See Plate 72.) Although produced in the Karabagh area, these rugs possess features that are reminiscent of both Kazak and Karabagh. Opinions differ on the exact classification of these rugs as either Karabaghs or Kazaks. The general consensus is that they should be considered to be Karabaghs.

PLATE 71: *KARABAGH ("Chelaberd" or "Eagle Kazak"),
5 ft. by 8 ft. Courtesy of Mr. and Mrs. Alan Johnson*

The Chondoresk (Cloudband or Dragon Kazak) is subject to the same classification controversy as the Chelaberd. Many features are characteristic of both Kazaks and Karabaghs, but it also should be classified as a Karabagh. The design has a medallion or medallions that contain cloudbands or dragon-like figures, which, in turn, surround a small geometric motif.

PLATE 72: *KARABAGH (Portion), 5 ft. by 9 ft. Courtesy of Hower House*

TALISH

KNOT: *Turkish*

WARP: *natural-colored wool*

WEFT: *natural-colored wool (occasionally dyed red or blue); double*

PILE: *medium*

FRINGE: *looped at one end; knotted at the other*

SELVEDGE: *blue wool over several warp threads*

Talish is a mountainous area on the Caspian Sea, south of the Moghan Steppe. It is directly south of Shirvan and east of Karabagh.

Talish rugs are easily identified by their characteristic design and shape. The field is usually navy, although red or cream is also used. The field may be open, or it may be filled with rosettes and/or stars; the field may even have only a single rosette or star. The main border is also a distinguishing mark of the Talish, almost always white with large rosettes separated by small squares or stars (see Plate 73). The vast majority of rugs produced are runners, with sizes ranging up to approximately 12 feet in length.

PLATE 73: *TALISH, 3 ft. by 6 ft. Courtesy of Hower House*

PLATE 74: *SHIRVAN, 3 ft. 5 in. by 6 ft.*
Courtesy of Russell Herbert

opposite, PLATE 75:
SHIRVAN
("Marasali" Prayer)
3 ft. by 4 ft.
Courtesy of
Mrs. Burch Thomas

SHIRVAN

KNOT:	*Turkish*
WARP:	*dark brown wool twisted with a single white strand*
WEFT:	*wool, white, or natural colored; occasionally cotton in newer rugs*
PILE:	*short*
FRINGE:	*looped at one end (often woven into a* kelim*); knotted at other*
SELVEDGE:	*several warp threads overcast with wool*

Vast numbers of rugs were woven in the Shirvan area in many different villages. As in the villages of Kuba, certain designs are woven that are unique to individual villages. Many different designs, such as large geometric medallions with eight-pointed stars or large, hooked octagons (see Plate 74), and many prayer rugs (see Plate 75) are found throughout the Shirvan area. One of the most unique designs is woven in the village of

Marasali: the field is filled with rows of pastel-colored *boteh*, each of which is encompassed by a serrated outline.

The Shirvan area is south of Kuba and southeast of the eastern slopes of the Greater Caucasus Mountain Range. The rugs of Shirvan are similar in color and design to those of Kuba, and are quite often mislabeled as Kabistans.

The most distinguishing feature of Shirvans is the warp thread. The three-ply warp is composed of two strands of dark brown wool that have entwined with a single strand of white wool. In addition, the warp threads lie horizontally to each other, as contrasted to the depressed warp threads of rugs from Kuba and Daghestan. This unique construction gives an almost flat appearance to the back of the rug.

The Shirvans are usually very finely knotted, with short pile. The colors tend to be more muted and subdued than in other Caucasian rugs.

BAKU

KNOT:	*Turkish*
WARP:	*brown wool*
WEFT:	*brown wool or a mixture of wool and cotton, double*
PILE:	*short*
FRINGE:	*knotted and cut at both ends*
SELVEDGE:	*blue wool or cotton over several warp threads*

Baku is the capital of the Soviet Republic of Azerbaijan. With a population of over one million people, Baku is the Soviet Union's fifth largest city. Located on the Aspheron Peninsula in the Caspian Sea, it is the center of the area's great oil industry.

The *boteh* is the design most often associated with the rugs of Baku. These *boteh* are of many different colors and the medallion (when used) is a pale blue. The colors used in Baku are more muted than those of other areas in the Caucasus. The rugs of the Baku area are noted for the many shades of blue used, from a light blue to a beautiful shade of turquoise. The ground is often a dark blue or black. The sizes tend to be small, and are rarely more than 6 feet by 9 feet.

Khila and Surahani have been the two most important Baku-area villages. The rugs of Khila contain a design with *boteh*, and the rugs of Surahani have a design that contains stars and rosettes. In Surahani, weaving is currently done in nationalized carpet factories. Traditional designs form the basis for the weaving. The sizes produced are typically 6 by 9 feet and smaller.

KUBA

KNOT:	*Turkish*
WARP:	*natural-colored wool or cotton*
WEFT:	*natural-colored wool or cotton*
PILE:	*short*
FRINGE:	*several rows of knots with cut fringe*
SELVEDGE:	*several warp threads overcast with blue or white wool*

The town of Kuba lies near the Caspian Sea, halfway between Derbend and Baku. Rugs are made in a number of villages in the Kuba area, each of which tends to weave its own design. (For example: Sejshour weaves a design with large diagonal cross beams in the field of the rug; Perepedil weaves a design which resembles a ram's head.) As a result, there is no single design that distinguishes a Kuba from other Caucasian rugs.

An important differentiating feature is the narrow *kelims* at both ends of the rug that are reinforced with a blue Soumak stitch. The Kuba rugs are generally finely woven, and possess a thick foundation because of alternating warp threads that are depressed into the body of the rug. (See Plate 76.)

Chi-Chi was the most prolific of the Kuba-area villages. The size of its field tends to be restricted because of the numerous borders used. Small stepped, hooked polygons situated in rows adorn the field of the rug.

PLATE 76: *KUBA*
4 ft. by 6 ft.
Courtesy of
Mrs. William
Campbell, Sr.

DAGHESTAN

KNOT:	*Turkish*
WARP:	*natural-colored wool or cotton*
WEFT:	*natural-colored wool or cotton*
PILE:	*medium to medium long*
FRINGE:	*three or four rows of knots with cut fringe at both ends*
SELVEDGE:	*warp overcast with blue wool*

The Daghestan area, now the Soviet state of Daghestan, occupies the northeast slopes of the Greater Caucasus Mountains. It is the northernmost of the Caucasian rug-producing areas.

Enormous numbers of prayer rugs were woven with a cream-colored field filled with small geometrical flowers contained in a trellis. Another design quite common to Daghestan is that of diagonal bands containing small hooked motifs and covering the entire field of the rug. Many of these rugs have been confused with Shirvans and Kubas, and a careful study of the structure should be made before classification of a rug. Rugs currently made in the Daghestan area contain bold, geometric medallions and employ small motifs scattered throughout the field (see Plate 77).

The body of Daghestan rugs is quite thick because of the depression of alternating warp threads into the body of the rug. The warp threads have a distinctive knotting characteristic of three or four rows of knots, giving a honeycomb effect, before the cut fringe at the ends.

DERBEND

KNOT:	*Turkish*
WARP:	*wool, cotton, or a mixture of both*
WEFT:	*wool, two or three strands*
PILE:	*heavy wool, medium long*
FRINGE:	*knotted at both ends*
SELVEDGE:	*two warp threads overcast with blue wool*

Located on the coast of the Caspian Sea, the town of Derbend is surrounded by the Daghestan area. In general, the rugs of Derbend were inferior to those of the whole of Daghestan. They were loosely woven with dark colors, navy blue and madder red. Repeated small geometric motifs or three geometric medallions were often used in Derbend designs; however, a variety of designs were used.

RECENT CAUCASIAN RUGS FROM THE SOVIET UNION

Today, most of the weaving from the Caucasus areas of the Soviet Union is done in government factories and workshops scattered throughout the Soviet Republics of Azerbaijan, Armenia, and Daghestan. These rugs, like those woven in the Turkomen Republic, are marketed in Moscow by Novoexport.

	KNOTS PER SQUARE METER	KNOTS PER SQUARE INCH
AZERBAIJANIAN CARPETS		
Kuba-Shirvan Quality	350,000	226
Kazakh-Karabakh Quality	160,000	103
ARMENIAN CARPETS		
Kuba-Shirvan Quality	200,000	129
Kazakh-Karabakh Quality	160,000	103
Erevan Quality	200,000	129
DAGHESTANIAN CARPETS		
Mikrakh Quality	194,000	194
Derbent Quality	116,000	116

CHART 1: *QUALITY GRADES OF CAUCASIAN RUGS FROM THE SOVIET UNION*

A new Caucasian rug is labeled with the name of the republic in which it was woven—Azerbaijan, Armenia, or Daghestan. These carpets are further classified by quality designations based on their number of knots per square meter. Novoexport uses the names of traditional Caucasian weaving areas for the various quality grades. These designations refer only to the quality of the carpet, not where it was woven, nor the design which it may possess. For example, a rug of Kuba-Shirvan quality is just as likely to have a Kazak design as it is to have a Shirvan or Kuba design. The quality of the carpet is determined primarily by the knot count; quality grades range from 150,000 to 300,000 knots per square meter (103 to 194 knots per square inch). See Chart 1. If the quality label is absent at the time of purchase, it is quite easy to determine the quality (and hence the category) of the carpet by counting the number of knots per square inch and referring to Chart 1.

The highly engineered looms used currently in Soviet weaving allow an even tension to be maintained during the weaving process. The new Caucasian carpets have a more regular shape than those older Caucasian carpets, which were woven on more primitive looms.

Chrome dyes are used in most current Soviet weaving, allowing a wide range of color combinations. The dyes are colorfast and will not fade when washed or exposed to sunlight. Armenian carpets are given a light chemical wash before they are exported; the carpets of Azerbaijan and Daghestan are exported unwashed.

Caucasian carpets are woven in a variety of sizes ranging from 60 to 90 centimeters (roughly 2 by 3 feet) to room-size carpets. Larger sizes, defined by Novoexport as measuring more than 4.5 square meters (approximately 50 square feet), and runners are available and are priced slightly higher per square meter than the smaller sizes.

6

Turkoman Rugs

THE VAST AREA referred to as Turkestan receives its name from the people of Turkic stock, called Turkomans, who have inhabited the region since 500 A.D. For centuries, trade routes through Turkestan have linked the Far East with Europe. The riches of China were brought to Europe by Marco Polo as early as 1295 A.D. Turkestan has had little direct influence on Europe and the western world, although its land has had a long history of conquest. In the fourth century B.C., Alexander the Great was the first in a series of famous conquerors who subjugated Turkestan. Genghis Khan ruled its large expanses in the thirteenth century, and Tamerlane established the capital of his great Mongol Empire at Samarkand in the fourteenth century. Russia's gradual conquest of Turkestan began in the seventeenth century; by the middle of the nineteenth century most of western Turkestan was under Russian rule. For the most part of the nineteenth century eastern Turkestan was under Chinese rule.

In the past, Turkoman rugs were woven in the vast area of central Asia that extends from the Gobi Desert in China on the east, to the Caspian Sea on the west. The Kazakh Steppe in the Soviet Republic of Kazakh bounds the area on the north; Iran's Kopet Dagh Mountains and Afghanistan's Hindu Kush and Paropamisus Mountains are the southern limits (see Figure 19).

The many tribes of this region have traditionally been nomadic and virtually unaffected by political boundaries. This way of life changed in the early 1930s, when the Russians established, and began to strictly enforce, the Soviet borders. After the vast majority of Turkestan land fell under Soviet control, the nomadic Turkoman could no longer freely migrate and thus was forced to change his traditional life-style.

Currently, Turkoman rugs are woven in Afghanistan, northeast Iran, and the Soviet Republic of Turkmenia. In Iran, Turkoman carpets are woven in the Persian Steppe by a few tribes of Tekke and Yomud;

these carpets are marketed in Tehran and regionally in Mashad. Carpets woven by the Soviet Turkomen are marketed in Moscow by Novoexport, which also markets the Caucasian carpets. The majority of the Soviet Turkoman carpets are exported to the European markets; the extremely high duty imposed on Soviet carpets by the United States tends to limit their importation to the American market.

Turkoman rugs now are labeled with their country of origin, as are all recently woven Oriental rugs. This practice has deemphasized the classification of these carpets by specific tribal origin. Instead, they are identified by the broader term "Turkoman."

Turkoman rugs are unmistakable in design; geometric motifs, *guls* unique to each tribe, are repeated in rows throughout the field of the rug. Figure 20 shows the most commonly encountered major *guls* (motifs).

The major variation to the repeated-*gul* design of Turkoman rugs is that of the *hatchlou* (or *katchli*), most often woven by members of the Yomud, Tekke, and Ersari (Afghan) tribes. In the *hatchlou* design, the field is divided into quadrants by two perpendicular strips or bars, resulting in a cross-like form (see Plate 78).

The quadrants are filled either with motifs resembling candlesticks or candelabras (Tekke or Ersari), or with small lozenge shapes (Yomud). The motifs contained in the bars and borders of the *hatchlou* design are characteristic of those associated with the rug's tribal origins. Rug dealers

FIGURE 19: *TURKOMAN TRIBAL LOCATIONS*

tend to label all Turkoman-*gul* rugs regardless of age as Bukharas* whether they are from Pakistan, Afghanistan, Iran, or the Soviet Union. Repeated-*gul* designs are termed "Royal Bukharas"; *hatchlou* designs are called "Princess Bukharas." Few if any rugs were woven in Bukhara; the town was simply a marketplace for the rugs of several of the Turkoman tribes.

Like the nomadic women of Iran, Turkoman women weave their rugs on horizontal or ground looms. The warp and weft threads are of wool or goat's hair, or a mixture of both. The pile is generally a good-quality wool or camel's hair. Most Turkoman rugs are woven with the Persian knot;

---

* Alternate spellings are Bukara and Bokhara.

PLATE 78: *HATCHLOU DESIGN–TEKKE (with Prayer Arch)*

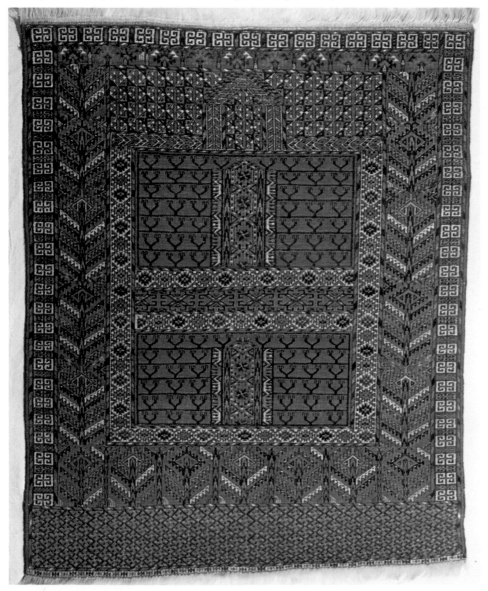

FIGURE 20: *MAJOR TURKOMAN GULS*

however, the Sarik and Yomud tribes predominately used the Turkish knot. Red is the dominant color, with specific shade varying from tribe to tribe.

Turkoman weavers were not averse to the use of aniline dyes, and some semi-antique Turkomans exhibit the characteristic signs of fading associated with these dyes. Proper caution should be used (see Dyes, pp. 22-23).

Antique Turkoman rugs are rare. Semi-antique Turkomans are not widely available, but may be encountered. Because of their increased popularity, new Turkoman rugs are widely available on the western markets.

SALOR

KNOT: *Persian*
WARP: *light-colored wool or goat's hair*
WEFT: *light-colored wool, single or double*
PILE: *short, tightly knotted, fine-quality wool*
FRINGE: *narrow* kelim *with plain fringe*
SELVEDGE: *double overcast with wool*

The Salor tribe was once the wealthiest and most prestigious of the Turkoman tribes. They occupied the oasis land surrounding Merv from the late seventeenth century until driven from their homelands by the Tekke tribe in 1856. By 1870, tribal wars and disputes had dispersed the Salor population, and many Salors were absorbed into Sariq and Tekke tribes. A small group of Salors still reside around Marutshak in northern Afghanistan.*

The Salor *gul* is octagonal with spiked projections pointing both inward and outward from its rim. A smaller octagon appears at the center of the *gul*. The secondary *guls* used in Salor rugs resemble the major *guls* of the Tekke and Sariq tribes. The colors used vary from a rose wine to a mahogany. The Salor tribe used the finest-quality wool, and their weaving technique was the best of all the Turkoman tribes. (See Plate 79.)

A Salor-like *gul* is woven in Afghanistan today by Sariq tribes. The rugs in which these *guls* appear resemble the traditional Sariq rugs in colors and skirt ornamentation, and are marketed as Sariq Mauri.

---

* Eiland, Murray, *Oriental Rugs: A Comprehensive Guide* (Greenwich, Conn.: New York Graphic Society, Ltd., 1976), p. 144.

PLATE 79: *SALOR Chuval (Bag Face) 2 ft. by 4 ft. Courtesy of Dr. and Mrs. John Campbell*

SARIQ *(Saryk, Sarik)*

KNOT:	*Turkish, occasionally Persian*
WARP:	*wool with alternating warp threads slightly depressed*
WEFT:	*wool, double*
PILE:	*medium short wool*
FRINGE:	*wide* kelim *with plain fringe at both ends*
SELVEDGE:	*double, often overcast with alternating dark blue and red wool, giving a checkered appearance*

Since the late nineteenth century, a group of Sariq tribes have lived along the Murghab River south of Merv (in the Pinde district), around Marutshak; another group resides between Maimana and Qaisar. With the gradual dispersal of the Salor tribes after the fall of Merv in 1856, many Salors made new homes among the Sariq tribes. These Salors continued to weave their *guls* while probably adopting some of the Sariq weaving characteristics, which adds to the confusion of trying to pinpoint an exact tribal identification. Currently in Afghanistan, Sariq tribes weave a rug with a Salor *gul* and Sariq structural characteristics. See Sariq Mauri, p. 122.

The Sariq *gul* has an octagon shape similar to that of the Tekke. The *gul* is generally divided into quadrants with the center of the *gul* containing a cross-like motif. The secondary *guls* resemble those used by the Tekke. Sariq rugs were deep purplish brown, colors darker than those used in most Turkoman rugs. (See Plate 80.)

YOMUD *(Yomut)*

KNOT:	*Turkish, occasionally Persian*
WARP:	*wool or goat's hair, white or light colored*
WEFT:	*wool, double (single in new Iranian Yomuds)*
PILE:	*wool*
FRINGE:	*wide* kelim *with either braided or plain fringe*
SELVEDGE:	*double overcast with wool*

At the beginning of the nineteenth century, the Yomud tribes resided along the eastern shores of the Caspian Sea. Since then, the many Yomud tribes have separated and become widely scattered over northeast Iran, Afghanistan, and Russia. Even though this dispersal has caused a greater variation in the Yomud designs than those of other Turkoman tribes, most of the Yomud *guls* retain their characteristic latch hook. This distinctive ornamentation reflects the Yomud's original proximity to the Caucasus region, where the use of the latch hook is so prevalent. Since World War II, the Yomud tribes living in Iran have woven not only the traditional Yomud *gul* but also a Tekke-type *gul.*

The Yomud *gul* is a diamond-shaped motif with latched or serrated edges (see Plate 81). The *gul* may be divided into quarters; the size of the *gul* varies from tribe to tribe. In addition to the traditional Turkoman *gul* designs, a *hatchlou* design rug, without an arch, is also woven by Yomuds (see Plate 82). At the ends of Yomud rugs, between the borders and the *kelim,* are wide bands or skirts woven with a slightly different design from that which is used in the side borders. These skirts are decorated with a wide variety of designs.

The reds used by Yomud tribes vary from reddish brown to a wine red.

PLATE 81: *YOMUD*
6 ft. 3 in. by 4 ft. 4 in.

PLATE 82: *YOMUD (Hatchlou Design) 4 ft. by 5 ft. Courtesy of Mrs. Burch Thomas*

White is generally used in the primary border and appears more often in Yomuds than in other Turkoman rugs.

Sizes vary greatly according to use; many saddlebags and tent bags as well as room-size rugs are available. The antique and semi-antique pieces are rare, but recent examples of Yomud weaving are available on the market.

TEKKE

KNOT: *Persian*
WARP: *wool*
WEFT: *wool or goat's hair, double*
PILE: *short, fine-quality wool*
FRINGE: *narrow* kelim, *usually red with small motifs*
SELVEDGE: *double overcast with wool usually dyed navy blue*

In the last half of the nineteenth century, Tekke tribes occupied the Akhal and the Merv Oases (now located in the Soviet Republic of Turkmenia),

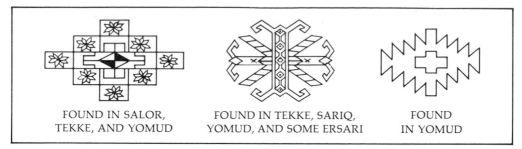

| FOUND IN SALOR, TEKKE, AND YOMUD | FOUND IN TEKKE, SARIQ, YOMUD, AND SOME ERSARI | FOUND IN YOMUD |

FIGURE 21: *MINOR TURKOMAN GULS*

as well as most of the land in between. The Russians defeated the Tekke tribes at Merv in 1884, and many Tekke tribes migrated south into Afghanistan. Border controls were tightened in 1930, making further migration impossible.

The distinguishing characteristic of the Tekke rug is its *gul,* an octagonal motif divided symmetrically into quadrants. Each *gul* contains an eight-pointed design (although a six-pointed design is often used in newer rugs) emitting spiked projections. Each *gul* is usually connected to neighboring *guls* by horizontal and vertical lines, which run through the field of the carpet. Spider-like minor, or secondary, *guls* occupy the spaces between the rows and columns of the major Tekke *guls.* (See Figure 21.)

Today, weaving of the traditional Tekke *gul* is no longer limited to members of the Tekke tribe; it has recently been woven in Iran by several Yomud tribes (the rugs of which are called Bukharas or, more generally, Turkomans), in Afghanistan by Sariq and Ersari tribes (whose Tekke-*gul* rugs are referred to as Mauri; see pp. 121-122), and in Pakistan (whose Turkoman-*gul* rugs are also termed Bukharas). The Tekke *gul* is the one used most often in those Bukhara rugs that are woven in Pakistan.

The Tekke rugs of Iran are usually woven with a woolen warp and weft. The Tekke rugs made in Afghanistan have a fine white or light-colored wool used for both the warp and weft threads. The pile of the Tekke rugs made in both Iran and Afghanistan is excellent-quality, hard-wearing wool.

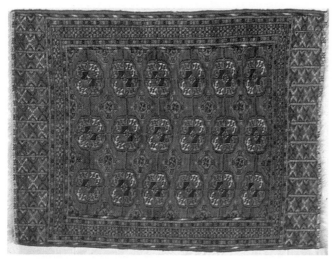

PLATE 83: *TEKKE, 3 ft. 5 in. by 4 ft. 5 in.*

117

Three borders generally surround the field of the rug; the center, wider border contains a series of octagonal shapes. Outside the borders, at the top and at the bottom of a Tekke rug, will be a wide panel or skirt, usually containing a hooked diamond motif. Ground colors are either a brick red or a dark wine. White, burnt orange, and dark blue are the most common motif colors. (See Plate 83.)

The Tekke is the most prevalent of the antique and semi-antique Turkoman rugs. They can be found with either the Tekke *gul* or the *hatchlou* ("cross") design in 3 by 5 to 4 by 6 feet sizes as well as saddlebags and bag faces. New Tekke rugs come in a wide variety of sizes.

ERSARI

KNOT:	*Persian (several rows of Turkish knots are often found*
WARP:	*gray-colored wool or goat's hair*
WEFT:	*dark-colored wool of goat's hair, double*
PILE:	*thick, excellent-quality wool*
FRINGE:	*wide kelim usually red, with knotted fringe at both ends*
SELVEDGE:	*selvedge overcast with dark-colored wool or goat's hair*

For several hundred years Ersari tribes have lived along the banks of the Amu Darya, a river which forms a portion of the boundary between Afghanistan and the Soviet Union. Ersari tribes could be found as far north as Chardzhou (160 miles inside the Soviet Union) and scattered throughout northeast Afghanistan. Although clans of Ersari have resided in Afghanistan since the late seventeenth century, mass migrations of Ersari occurred from 1874, when Khiva fell to the Russians, to the closing of the Russo-Afghan border in the early 1930s.

As a result, the Ersaris constitute the largest Turkoman population in Afghanistan today. Important to the Afghanistan economy, Ersaris are the principal rug-weaving tribes, as well as a significant factor in sheepherding. Sheepskin and carpets are Afghanistan's major exports.

Ersari rugs usually possess a typical Turkoman-style *gul* design. The most common of the many Ersari *guls* is a quartered octagon encompassing a polygon; each quadrant contains at least one dog-shaped motif. Yet Ersaris weave a wide variety of designs, ranging from the geometric and bold *filpoi* ("elephant's foot") *gul* of the "Afghan," to the floral and the Herati pattern of the Beshire.

The Persian is the primary knot used by the Ersari tribes. In many Ersari carpets, every other warp thread is slightly depressed. The selvedges are often double and overcast with goat's hair, in fashion similar to those of the Balouchi tribes. Ersari rugs are brighter in color than most of other

Turkoman rugs; yellow and blue predominate as secondary colors. (See Plate 84.)

The sizes of Ersari rugs vary from small mat and bag faces to room size. The antique Ersari are rather rare. Although not common, the semi-antique Ersari rugs are more easily obtained. For the new production of the Ersari, see the section, *Recent Turkoman Rugs of Afghanistan*, pp. 121-123.

PLATE 84: *ERSARI (Antique), 2 ft. by 4 ft. Courtesy of Mrs. Clair Harrah*

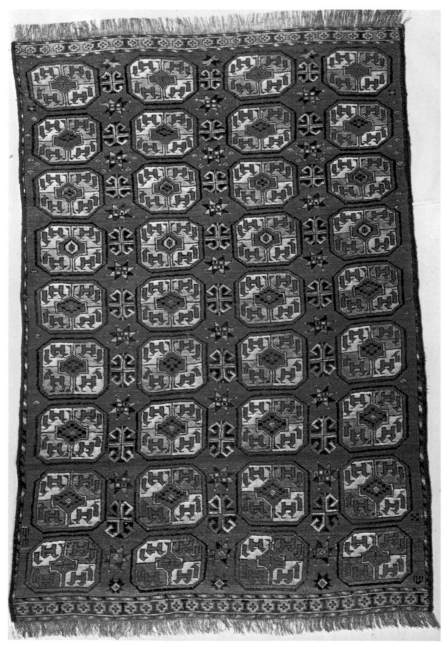

AFGHAN

Afghan rugs were made by Ersari tribes regardless of location of the weavers (either Afghanistan or Soviet Union). "Afghan" refers to design (the *gul* motif), rather than country of origin.

Afghan rugs have either a single column or several columns of repeated *filpoi* ("elephant's foot") *guls*. The *filpoi* is a large octagonal *gul*, which may range in diameter from 10 to 15 inches. Each *gul* is quartered, with each segment containing a trefoil or treelike design. The trefoils extend from a central polygon or square. The same *filpoi* design used in the Afghan is also used in a rug called the Khiva. The only difference between the Afghan and the Khiva is in quality; the Khiva is more finely woven.

Wool warp and weft threads are used. Often the wool is from goats rather than sheep. The pile is a good-quality heavy wool that has been knotted with the Persian knot.

The ground of most Afghans is a deep red with designs outlined in black, dark blue, or brown (see Plate 85). In recent years, a "golden Afghan" has appeared on the market. Some of these rugs were originally red, but were heavily bleached to obtain a yellow hue. A careful inspection of the base of the pile will reveal remnants of the original red color. The bleached wool has been weakened and the wearing qualities impaired, so caution should be exercised in buying. True "golden Afghans" are woven with yellow yarn and possess the same excellent wearing qualities of the red Afghans.

Afghans are solid, durable rugs that are relatively inexpensive. They are available in virtually all sizes.

PLATE 85: *AFGHAN*
(Portion)
6 ft. by 9 ft.
Courtesy of Mr. and
Mrs. Ted Trikilis

RECENT TURKOMAN RUGS
OF AFGHANISTAN

Rugs made in Afghanistan since World War II are classified in a way different from the semi-antique and antique Turkoman rugs. They are indeed Turkoman rugs, but further classification is necessary for several reasons. First, during the border disputes, there were many migrations and resettlings of the Turkoman tribes and their subtribes. Remnants of one tribe often merged with those of another, finally settling outside each of their traditional homelands. Although these Turkomans continued weaving rugs, they often adopted and adapted the antique *guls*. For example, a Tekke-*design* rug not woven by a Tekke tribe is labeled *Mauri* rather than Tekke. Second, new designs have emerged, owing to their increased popularity as well as the commercial motive of weaving designs to meet consumer tastes.

There are two principal types of Turkoman rugs woven in Afghanistan today. The Mauri is an excellent-quality carpet, usually with a Tekke *gul* design. (See Plate 86.) The Daulatabad, also a fine-quality rug, is woven with the *filpoi* design.

PLATE 86: *MAURI Courtesy of Fritz and LaRue Co.*

MAURI

KNOT: *Persian*
WARP: *wool (white or light gray)*
WEFT: *dark wool*
PILE: *short, evenly clipped*
FRINGE: *wide* kelim *(may be red) with knotted fringe at both ends*
SELVEDGE: *overcast with dark blue or black wool*

Mauri rugs are woven in many areas throughout northern Afghanistan. Tekke-design Mauri rugs are woven in Marutshak, Mazar-i-Sharif, and Herat and its surrounding province. Several carpets with other *guls* are also given the Mauri label. For example, the Sariq Mauri, woven primarily by the Sariq tribe, has a Salor-like *gul*, Sariq colors, and skirt designs reminiscent of antique Sariq rugs.

DAULATABAD

KNOT: *Persian*
WARP: *gray wool (may vary from light to dark)*
WEFT: *dark brown or black wool*
PILE: *medium to medium long, heavy coarse wool*
FRINGE: *wide* kelim *(usually red) with knotted fringe at both ends*
SELVEDGE: *double selvedge overcast with dark wool*

PLATE 87: *DAULATABAD (Prayer Design), 3 ft. by 5 ft. Courtesy of Dr. and Mrs. John Campbell*

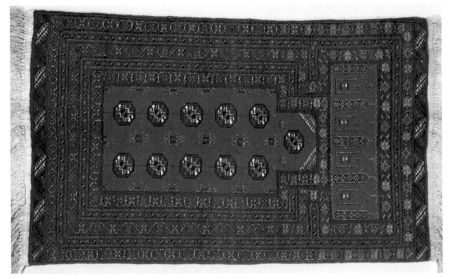

Like the Mauri rugs, the Daulatabads are made in various weaving centers throughout northern Afghanistan. They too may be typed according to the various adaptations in the *gul* design. (See Plate 87.)

The majority of all Turkoman rugs now being woven are made in Afghanistan. The focus of our discussion of Afghanistan Turkomans has been the Mauri and Daulatabad, since these excellent-quality rugs comprise the majority of the rug production for the U.S. market. Mauri and Daulatabad are not representative of all Afghanistani weaving; medium- and lower-quality rugs are being produced in Aktsha and Shibergan. Much of the weaving comes from numerous small subtribes and families; these rugs have not been discussed because of their great variation and individually insignificant production.

Excellent-quality Turkoman rugs are being woven across the Afghan border in the Soviet republics of Turkmen and Uzbek; few are found on the U.S. market because of the extremely high (45 percent) duty imposed. The current rug production of the Yomud and Tekke tribes of northeast Iran has been discussed previously in the respective sections.

EASTERN TURKESTAN *(Xinjiang)*

KNOT:	*Persian, Turkish (in older rugs)*
WARP:	*cotton*
WEFT:	*cotton, wool (in older rugs); two or more*
PILE:	*soft, silky wool*
FRINGE:	kelim *with looped fringe at one end and* kelim *with plain fringe at the other*
SELVEDGE:	*overcast with wool*

The Tien Shan Mountains separate Eastern and Western Turkestan. Often called Chinese Turkestan, Eastern Turkestan is located in what is now Xinjiang, an autonomous region in the People's Republic of China.

The rugs of Eastern Turkestan reflect a unique combination of Chinese, Turkoman, and Caucasian influences. This unique blending of designs and motifs gives these rugs an appearance strikingly different from the rugs of other weaving areas.

The rugs of Khotan often have a medallion that resembles a flattened disc; the medallion in turn may contain several smaller motifs. This medallion, called *Ay Gul* (moon motif), may appear in single, double, or even triple forms. (See Plate 88.) A pattern reminiscent of the Persian Tree-of-life design is also commonly woven in the rugs of Yarkand, Khotan, and Kashgar. This design is actually of a pomegranate tree bearing fruit; the tree is usually located at the base of the field.

PLATE 88: *KHOTAN, 6 ft. by 9 ft. Courtesy of Dr. Theodore Herbert*

The prayer design used in this area is woven in the *saff* form, that of multiple prayer *mihrabs* (niches). The fields of the *mihrabs* are either empty or, more often, filled with the pomegranate-tree design.

The colors in some of the older rugs were considered harsh. An orange-red was the dominant color used in the ground; a golden-yellow tone and several shades of blue were used for the motifs. Other carpets had more muted tones, such as peach, light blue, gray, steel blue, brown, and gold colors. The newer carpets of Xinjiang have a pleasing combination of different shades of blue, brown, cream, and shades of rose red.

The weave of antique carpets from Eastern Turkestan was rather coarse; the wool used was soft and not very durable. Consequently, many of these rugs did not withstand wear very well. Carpets currently woven in Xinjiang are much more finely woven, of either a 90-line or 110-line quality; this aspect will be discussed later in Chapter 8. Xinjiangs have a much thicker and heavier pile, yielding a much sturdier carpet than their earlier counterparts. The warp and weft threads of all new rugs are cotton; wool was used for the weft threads in many older rugs. For more information on these rugs, see *Affordable Oriental Rugs.**

---

* Janice Summers Herbert, *Affordable Oriental Rugs* (New York: Macmillan Publishing Co., Inc., 1980).

Turkish Rugs

CARPETS FROM TURKEY were among the first Oriental carpets to reach Europe. Known as "Turkey carpets," they were depicted in European paintings as early as the fourteenth century. In the fifteenth and sixteenth centuries, paintings by such artists as Holbein, Lotto, and Carpaccio employed Turkish carpets. In these paintings, Turkish carpets decorate balustrades and are used as table as well as floor coverings.

During the nineteenth century, Turkish carpets dominated western rug markets. Prior to World War I, over half of all Turkish rugs woven were of the prayer design. Most rugs were woven with rectilinear designs and motifs. The exceptions were the rugs from the few weaving areas that specialized in "court carpet" production. Court carpets were quite sophisticated, using much more formal design elements. Design forms were curvilinear, rather than the usual rectilinear; extensive use was made of cloudbands, palmettes, and arabesques. Animal and human figures are rarely found in Turkish carpets. The Sunnite Moslem weavers of Turkey were strict in their interpretation of the Koranic prohibition against depicting human and animal forms.

After proclaiming the Turkish Republic in 1923, Kemal Ataturk began a program of industrialization and westernization. The changes brought about by the rapid industrialization were coupled with natural disasters and political upheavals in the early 1920s. These caused a dramatic downturn in the Turkish carpet industry, which lasted almost fifty years. Although weaving continued on a smaller scale than before by villagers and nomads throughout the country, it has been only recently that the industry has begun to recover.

Most Turkish carpets are named for the village or town in which they are woven; however, carpets woven in very small villages often are labeled instead with the name of the town in which they are marketed. Yet there

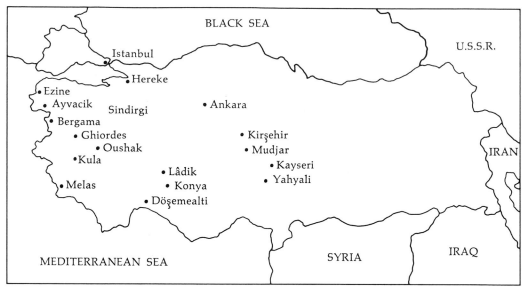

FIGURE 22: *MAJOR RUG-WEAVING CENTERS OF TURKEY*

are many nomadic tribes that inhabit the Anatolian plateau. Collectively these tribes are called Yürük, and the carpets woven by these tribespeople are called Yürüks.

HEREKE

KNOT:	*Turkish*
WARP:	*cotton; silk*
WEFT:	*cotton; silk*
PILE:	*wool; silk*
FRINGE:	*small* kelim *with knotted fringe at both ends*
SELVEDGE:	*single, overcast with wool or silk*

The small town of Hereke is located at the eastern end of the Sea of Marmara, approximately forty miles (65 km) east of Istanbul. The weavers of Hereke are known for making some of the world's finest carpets.

Two types of carpets are woven in Hereke. One type has wool pile, and is woven with cotton warp and weft threads; the other has silk pile, and is woven with silk warp and weft threads. The wool-pile carpets are woven in large sizes, which range from 6 by 9 feet (approximately 2 by 3 meters) to room-size. Silk-pile carpets are woven in smaller sizes, the largest being 4 by 6 feet (approximately 1.5 by 2 meters).

The weavers of Hereke use a variety of designs, many of which have been adopted from other Turkish and Persian weaving centers. Hereke designs are curvilinear, with numerous arabesques, cloudbands, vines, and

tendrils filling the field. The design most characteristic of the Hereke is
that of a prayer rug with a *mihrab* having a distinctive head-neck-and-
shoulders appearance. The head portion is usually quite large, restricting
the area of the field. A small cartouche containing Arabic script is usually
present in the upper portion of the arch. In many silk rugs, the motifs are
accentuated by gold threads in a soumak stitch, which gives a relief effect
to the pile. The inscription "HEREKE" in the western alphabet often appears in a border cartouche.

The rugs of Hereke are tightly woven and their quality is excellent.
This is reflected in their prices: they are rather expensive.

EZINE

KNOT:	*Turkish*
WARP:	*wool, light colored*
WEFT:	*wool, dyed red; two or more*
PILE:	*long, shaggy wool*
FRINGE:	*very wide* kelim *with decorative stripe and plain fringe*
SELVEDGE:	*triple, overcast with wool*

Approximately thirty miles (50 km) south of the western Turkish town
of Çanakkale is the city of Ezine. Rugs called Ezines are woven in the
many small villages that surround the city.

The designs found in Ezines fall into two categories. In one, a strong

Caucasian influence may be observed in the designs and motifs. The large stepped medallion, capped on the top and bottom by a triangular arch, dominates the field. The use of small octagons containing multicolored stepped polygons and serrated-leaf major borders, common to many Caucasian rugs, are typical of this type of Ezine.

In the second type of Ezine, the designs have been borrowed from the Turkish weaving center of Bergama. In the Bergama-influenced rugs, the most commonly used design is a field divided into two squares; these squares contain either stepped polygons within an octagon or rectangles with arrows protruding from each side.

Red is used for the field; yellow, blue, and white are used for the designs and motifs. The majority of Ezines are small, approximately 3 feet 4 inches by 4 feet 8 inches (100 by 143 cm).

AYVACIK

KNOT:	*Turkish*
WARP:	*wool, light colored*
WEFT:	*wool, dyed red; two or more*
PILE:	*long, shaggy wool*
FRINGE:	*wide red* kelim *with knotted fringe at both ends*
SELVEDGE:	*triple, overcast with wool*

The small town of Ayvacik is located approximately seventeen miles (30 km) southeast of Ezine. Carpets woven in both Ayvacik and Ezine usually are marketed in Çanakkale; they often are sold under the Çanakkale name.

Rugs from Ayvacik are quite similar to those of Ezine in structure, although Ayvaciks generally are not woven as finely as Ezines.* The designs and motifs used in Ayvacik reflect the same Caucasian influence found in many Ezines.

One of the most common designs is a long, narrow hexagon that dominates the central field; the ends of the hexagon terminate in a pair of hooked protrusions resembling ice tongs. A column of small octagonal or star-shaped motifs flanks the hexagon. The field is often a rich golden-yellow color, while white, red, blue, and green are used for the motifs.

---

* J. Iten-Maritz, *Turkish Carpets* (Tokyo: Kodansha International, 1975), p. 94.

PLATE 90: *BERGAMA, 3 ft. 6 in. by 4 ft. 2 in.*
Courtesy of Mori S.A.

BERGAMA

KNOT:	*Turkish*
WARP:	*wool*
WEFT:	*wool, dyed red; two or more*
PILE:	*medium long wool*
FRINGE:	*wide red* kelim *with plain fringe*
SELVEDGE:	*overcast with wool*

The town of Bergama is about thirty miles (50 km) east of the Aegean Sea. It is located on the site of the ancient Greek learning center of Pergamum. Carpets were woven here as early as the fourteenth century. The origins of many carpets depicted in the fifteenth- and sixteenth-century paintings of Holbein, Crivelli, and Carpaccio have been attributed to the Bergama area.

One of the most common designs of Bergama carpets is that of a large red diamond-shaped medallion superimposed on a navy blue field. The medallion is outlined with a chain of floral motifs. At the center of the medallion is a small geometric motif from which emanate twelve rays, giving the appearance of a sunburst. Each of the four corner medallions contains a small geometric rosette.

Bergama carpets are small and tend to be squarish in shape. They generally range in size from 2 feet 8 inches by 4 feet 4 inches to 3 feet 8 inches by 5 feet 6 inches (80 by 130 cm to 110 by 165 cm).

KOZAK

KNOT:	*Turkish*
WARP:	*wool*
WEFT:	*wool, two to four*
PILE:	*medium*
FRINGE:	*wide* kelim *containing striped bands and plaited fringe*
SELVEDGE:	*triple, overcast with red wool*

Kozak is a small town about twelve miles (20 km) north of Bergama. Rugs woven here have bold geometric designs and brilliant colors, resembling the Caucasian Kazaks.

Prayer and medallion designs are those most commonly used by the weavers of Kozak. In the medallion-design carpets, a large square is centered in the field. This medallion is either a plain square or a square with arched protrusions at its top and bottom. Prayer-design Kozaks generally have open fields, across which may be dispersed several geometric motifs.

The small round and octagonal motifs scattered throughout the field are quite similar to those woven in the rugs of Kazak. Floral motifs, resembling carnations, often are used for border motifs. Small triangles occasionally are woven in Kozak rugs, in the *kelim* as well as in the pile. These triangles, called *muskas*, are symbols of good luck.

Kozaks are brilliantly colored; shades of bright red, blue, green, and white most commonly are used. Green is used often for the color of the spandrel. In fact, Kozaks are notable for their use of the color green, and when the color is used, it occupies a greater proportion of the area of the rug than is common in Turkish rugs.

Kozaks are generally small, ranging in size from 2 feet 4 inches by 3 feet 7 inches to 3 feet 8 inches by 4 feet 2 inches (72 by 109 cm to 110 by 125 cm).

PLATE 91: *KOZAK (Prayer Design) 2 ft. 4 in. by 3 ft. 9 in. Courtesy of Mori S.A.*

PLATE 92: *YAĞCİBEDİR, 3 ft. 9 in. by 4 ft. 7 in.*
Courtesy of Mori S.A.

YAĞCİBEDİR

KNOT:	*Turkish*
WARP:	*wool, natural-colored*
WEFT:	*wool, double, dyed red*
PILE:	*medium short*
FRINGE:	*very wide* kelim *of colored bands with plaited fringe at both ends*
SELVEDGE:	*four, wool dyed navy blue*

Rugs called Yağcibedir are easily recognized by their characteristic blue field and red motifs. The most common design consists of a stepped hexagon superimposed on the field. A variety of small designs and motifs fill both the field and the area inside the hexagon.

The Yağcibedir rugs are woven in Sindirgi and surrounding villages. Unlike most Turkish rugs, which are named for the town or area in which they are woven, the Yağcibedirs take their name from the man who, according to legend, taught the area villagers the art of carpet weaving.

The wool used in these carpets is usually spun by hand and is of excellent quality. Warp threads are of natural-colored wool; weft threads are dyed red. The ends of the carpets are finished with a wide *kelim* of colored bands and plaited fringe. The Yağcibedirs are usually woven in small sizes; they range from approximately 2 feet 9 inches by 4 feet 6 inches (90 by 140 cm) to 3 feet 9 inches by 6 feet 6 inches (120 by 200 cm).

KULA

KNOT: *Turkish or Persian*
WARP: *wool; cotton in newer carpets*
WEFT: *wool; cotton in newer carpets*
PILE: *medium long, excellent-quality wool*
FRINGE: *small* kelim *with knotted fringe at both ends*
SELVEDGE: *overcast with wool*

Kula is located in central western Turkey. The town lies fifty miles (80 km) southeast of Ghiordes, between Izmir and Ushak. Carpets were woven here as early as the seventeenth century. Currently, however, very little weaving is done in the town of Kula itself; most weaving is done in the surrounding areas.

A wide variety of designs adopted from other weaving centers, as well as the centuries-old traditional designs, are woven in Kula. The most common Kula designs are the prayer rug and a medallion design. The typical prayer design employs an elongated *mihrab*, with an interior lined with small floral motifs. The central field is dominated either by a Tree-of-life or a floral spray hanging from the apex of the *mihrab*.

The medallion design used in Kula consists of a polygonal rectilinear medallion in the central field; the medallion often contains a smaller geometric motif. A variety of small floral motifs fill the rest of the field.

Older Kula rugs were woven with a woolen foundation; occasionally, however, cotton was substituted for the wool in the weft threads. Since World War II, the use of cotton for both the warp and weft threads has increased. The alternate warp threads are depressed, yielding a thicker-bodied carpet. When combined with the excellent-quality wool used for the pile, the depressed-warp technique yields a very durable carpet. Most Kulas are woven in small sizes, although room-size rugs are sometimes woven.

PLATE 93: *KULA*
(Prayer Design)
3 ft. 9 in. by 6 ft. 10 in.
Courtesy of
Polly Price Blake

PLATE 94: *MELAS*
(Prayer Design)
3 ft. 10 in. by 6 ft. 9 in.
Courtesy of Mori S.A.

MELAS *(Milas)*

KNOT:	*Turkish*
WARP:	*natural-colored wool; occasionally cotton*
WEFT:	*wool, two or more dyed red in older rugs and golden colored in newer rugs; occasionally cotton*
PILE:	*medium to medium long*
FRINGE:	kelim *with plain fringe at both ends*
SELVEDGE:	*double*

The town of Melas lies in the province of the same name, in southwestern Turkey. Carpets have been woven for several hundred years in Melas and in the surrounding villages.

A prayer design is indigenous to this area; a diamond-shaped lozenge is superimposed over the top of a prayer niche, giving a characteristic head-neck-and-shoulder appearance. The spandrel is ivory, and shades of red, brown, yellow, and ivory are used for the stylized motifs. In older carpets the prayer niche is dull brick red; in newer carpets, it is either reddish brown or brown.

The Ada Melas (commonly called "Melas stripe" or "Melas column") carpets are woven in the village of Karaova. The central field of these carpets is disproportionately small, being restricted by the unusually wide major border. The major border is composed of reciprocal salients, quite similar and often identical to each other. The central field design is often echoed in the border. The colors of Ada Melas are more muted than those other types of Melas.

The medallion design is also woven, although it is not as common as either the prayer design or the Ada Melas. A large central medallion is placed in a brilliant field. The field itself is somewhat restricted in size.

Melas carpets are coarsely woven on a woolen foundation. The pile is medium to medium long. Small sizes and runners are most common.

DÖŞEMEALTI

KNOT: *Turkish*
WARP: *natural-colored wool*
WEFT: *wool, two or more; dark colored*
PILE: *medium in length*
FRINGE: kelim *with plaited fringe at one end and looped fringe at the other*
SELVEDGE: *double*

Rugs referred to as Döşemealti are woven in Döşemealti and the plateaus around Anatalya. The wool used for the pile is shorn from the sheep of the area's plateaus and is of excellent quality. The most common design is a hexagonal field in which are contained small geometric motifs. Natural dyes are used; red and blue are the predominant colors. Döşemealti carpets are generally small, ranging in size from 2 feet 6 inches by 4 feet to 4 feet by 6 feet (75 by 120 cm to 120 by 180 cm); runners are also woven.

KONYA

KNOT: *Turkish*
WARP: *wool, natural colored*
WEFT: *wool, dyed red; two or more*
PILE: *medium, excellent-quality wool*
FRINGE: *wide* kelim *with plain fringe*
SELVEDGE: *triple, overcast with wool*

The Konya weaving district consists of the town of Konya and the villages of Lâdik, Karaman, Karapinar, Keçemuslu, Innice, Obruk, and Ergli. This district is one of Turkey's largest and most important rug-producing areas, producing rugs in a wide variety of designs.

Generally, Konya carpets are woven coarsely on a woolen foundation. Natural-colored wool is used for the warp and weft threads; the wefts usually are dyed red. The Konya district is noted for weaving a large number of prayer rugs; their fields are red, while gold and green are used for the designs and motifs. Medallion designs are also common; red and gold are the predominant colors used for the field and medallion.

PLATE 95: *DÖŞEMEALTI, 2 ft. 7 in. by 4 ft. 4 in.*
Courtesy of Mori S.A.

PLATE 96: *KONYA, 3 ft. 9 in. by 5 ft. 1 in.*
Courtesy of Mori S.A.

LÂDİK

KNOT:	*Turkish*
WARP:	*wool*
WEFT:	*wool, two or more*
PILE:	*short, excellent-quality wool*
FRINGE:	kelim *with plain fringe at both ends*
SELVEDGE:	*double, overcast with wool*

Lâdik is the most famous of the Konya-area villages. Until World War I, it was known for weaving prayer rugs with a characteristic "tulip" motif. The field of these rugs can be divided into three parts. The tulip motifs, with their long stalks, occupy the lower portion of the field, in a section divided from the *mihrab*. The *mihrab* comprises the center section, separating the spandrel and the tulip section. The *mihrab* may be empty, or filled with a hanging lamp or floral motif. The spandrels contain a stylized flower and a vessel on each side.

PLATE 97: *LÂDİK (Antique)*
3 ft. 7 in. by 6 ft. 9 in. Courtesy of Mori S.A.

KONYA-LÂDİK

KNOT:	*Turkish*
WARP:	*cotton*
WEFT:	*cotton, double*
PILE:	*medium, thick wool*
FRINGE:	*small* kelim *with knotted fringe at both ends*
SELVEDGE:	*overcast with wool*

The term Konya-Lâdik is used to refer to rugs currently woven in Lâdik. These rugs are different from those rugs woven in Lâdik prior to World War I. Konya-Lâdiks are woven on a cotton foundation with excellent-quality wool used for the pile. The most common designs used are floral and medallion patterns adopted from such Persian weaving centers as Tabriz.

YAHYALI

KNOT:	*Turkish*
WARP:	*natural-colored wool, occasionally cotton*
WEFT:	*wool, double*
PILE:	*medium to medium short*
FRINGE:	*small* kelim *with plain fringe*
SELVEDGE:	*double, overcast with navy blue wool*

Yahyali is located in south central Turkey. The majority of rugs from this area are woven by individuals in their homes; virtually every home has its

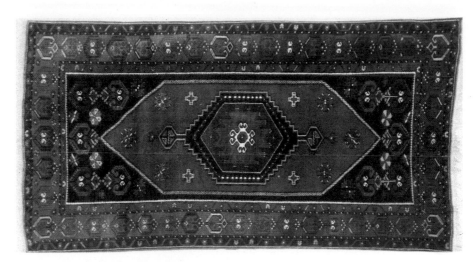

PLATE 98: *YAHYALI, 4 ft. by 7 ft. 5 in.*
Courtesy of Mori S.A.

own loom.* The design common to most Yahyali rugs is that of a central medallion superimposed on an elongated hexagon. Red and blue are the Yahyali's predominant colors, and are used for the field and central medallion.

Yahyalis are woven with a woolen foundation; the pile is of excellent-quality wool. Most Yahyalis are about 3 feet 6 inches by 7 feet (96 by 213 cm).

KAYSERİ

KNOT:	*Turkish*
WARP:	*cotton or silk*
WEFT:	*cotton or silk*
PILE:	*wool, silk, or artificial silk*
FRINGE:	kelim *with fringe at both ends*
SELVEDGE:	*double*

Long known by its Roman name, "Caesarea," Kayseri is located almost at the center of the Anatolian plateau. Carpets identified as "Kayseri" are woven in and around the town of Kayseri, as well as in the town of Bunyan. Although carpets have been woven in this area for centuries, Kayseri did not become one of Turkey's most important weaving centers until after World War II.

Kayseri carpets can be divided into three types, according to the ma-

---

* J. Iten-Maritz, *Turkish Carpets* (Tokyo: Kodansha International, 1975), p. 295.

PLATE 99: *KAYSERİ (Prayer Design)*
3 ft. 11 in. by 5 ft. 5 in.
Courtesy of Mori S.A.

terial used for the pile: wool, silk, and artificial silk. Wool-pile carpets are woven on a cotton foundation with excellent-quality wool.

Silk carpets are finely woven on a silk foundation. The silk used is excellent-quality Bursa silk. Like the silk Hereke rugs, Kayseri silks contain gold metallic threads that are used to accentuate certain designs and motifs. These threads are woven in a flatweave technique to give a relief effect.

Artificial silk (*ipekli*) is referred to also as "Kayseri floss." *Ipekli* carpets are woven on a cotton foundation; their pile is a blend of mercerized cotton and silk waste or rayon.* Carpets of this type do not withstand wear and should be used strictly for decorative purposes rather than as floor covering. Kayseri floss carpets are woven for export and the tourist trade. All too often they are sold as genuine silk carpets to unsuspecting tourists.

The designs woven in Kayseri carpets have been adopted from other weaving centers. Among the numerous designs used by the Kayseri weavers are the Ghiordes prayer, *saff*, and the Persian medallion and Hunting designs. Kayseri carpets are woven in all sizes; however, silk and Kayseri–floss carpets are generally woven in small sizes.

---

* J. Iten-Maritz, *Turkish Carpets* (Tokyo: Kodansha International, 1975), p. 252.

KIRŞEHIR

KNOT: *Turkish*
WARP: *wool*
WEFT: *wool, two or more*
PILE: *long, shaggy wool*
FRINGE: kelim *with fringe at both ends*
SELVEDGE: *double, overcast with wool*

Kirşehir lies in the heart of central Turkey, approximately halfway between Ankara and Kayseri. Carpets have been woven here for over two hundred years.

The most common designs used in Kirşehir are the medallion and prayer designs. In the medallion carpets, an elongated rectilinear medallion occupies the central field; the field itself may be either empty or filled, in a regimented form, with such small motifs as *boteh*. The length of the field is restricted at the top and bottom by a wide panel. The field of these carpets is often red; gold often is used for the main border color. A stylized lily-and-rosette design is commonly used as the main border design.

Most Kirşehirs are woven in small sizes, ranging up to approximately 3 feet 9 inches by 5 feet 9 inches (115 by 175 cm). Runners are also woven.

PLATE 100: *KIRŞEHIR, 3 ft. 6 in. by 5 ft. 3 in. Courtesy of Mori S.A.*

8 Rugs from China, India, and Pakistan

CHINA

KNOT:	*Persian*
WARP:	*cotton*
WEFT:	*cotton or silk, double*
PILE:	*medium to medium long wool or short silk*
FRINGE:	kelim *with knotted fringe at both ends*
SELVEDGE:	*overcast with wool or silk*

IN CHINA, THE WEAVING INDUSTRY operates under centralized government direction. Rugs are woven in seven major weaving centers or branches: Beijing, Tianjin, Shanghai, Hebei, Shandong, Dalein, and Xinjiang. Each of these branches has many workshops and factories, and each has its own specialized area of rug production.

Most Chinese rugs are woven with a woolen pile; this soft, lustrous wool comes from the western provinces. Some carpets are woven with goat, cow, or yak hair. Silk carpets may be woven on either a cotton or a silk foundation; cotton is used for the foundation of most other Chinese carpets.

Chinese carpets are often carved and sculptured. The designs and motifs to be sculptured are woven slightly longer than the rest of the carpet. The raised designs are accentuated further by being trimmed on the slant to give a relief or sculptured effect.

Line or knot count, type of wool, pile height, and type of weave are four major structural characteristics that are important in comparing the quality of Chinese carpets. The Chinese equivalent for knot count is *line* (see knot count, p. 163). A ninety-line rug has ninety knots per linear foot, which is equivalent to fifty-six knots per square inch. Line qualities commonly available are 70, 90, 120, and 240.

The wool used for the pile is either *machine-spun* or *hand-spun*. Most Chinese rugs are made of machine-spun wool, which is more even, uniform, and resilient than the hand-spun variety, yielding a more durable carpet.

Pile heights are measured in eighths of an inch, and are available in heights of 2/8, 3/8, 4/8, and 5/8 inch. Very finely knotted wool rugs (240 line or more) occasionally have a pile height only 2/8 inch. Silk rugs usually have 2/8-inch pile.

The appearance of the *back* of a carpet identifies the type of weave used: *open back* or *closed back*. Open-back rugs have weft threads that are clearly visible from the back; closed-back rugs have weft threads that are not visible because they are completely covered by the knots. Approximately twenty percent more wool is used in a closed-back rug than in a rug woven with an open back.

The most popular and common type of Chinese rug is known as the "Super Chinese," a 90-line, 5/8-inch-pile rug made with machine-spun wool and woven with a closed back. Chinese rug designs are not as elaborate and ornate as those from other weaving centers. They are well-proportioned with individual motifs, crisp and well-defined, due in part to the unique use of color. The Chinese are masters of the art of using graduated shades of the same color in their weaving. At times, as many as ten different shades of the same color are used in one rug.

Modern Chinese rugs are categorized, according to the nature of their designs, into four major groups. These classifications are Esthetic, Peking, Floral, and Self-tone Embossed.

PLATE 101: *GANSU (Semi-Antique) 2 ft. by 4 ft.*
Courtesy of Mrs. Russell Summers

Esthetic designs were adapted from those of seventeenth- and eighteenth-century French Savonnerie carpets. They are very formal in appearance; scalloped borders often surround a central medallion containing a large floral spray. (See Plate 102.)

Peking designs have been inspired by symbols of the Chinese heritage. Many of these designs and motifs can also be seen in other art forms such as sculpture, textiles, tiles, bronzes, and lacquer ware. (See Plate 103.)

Floral design rugs generally have no borders. Floral sprays and individual blossoms are scattered across the rug in such a fashion that they appear to be placed randomly.

PLATE 103: *PEKING DESIGN*
2 ft. 3 in. by 4 ft. 6 in.

PLATE 102: *ESTHETIC DESIGN*
3 ft. by 5 ft.
Courtesy of Polly Price Blake

The *Self-tone Embossed* design is also called the *Plain* design; as the name implies, these rugs are monochromatic. The designs and motifs of this type of carpet are either carved into or sculptured onto the pile, giving a relief effect.

Chinese rug designs are not unique to or characteristic of the village, tribe, or region where they are woven. As with other forms of Chinese art, rug designs were inspired by religious beliefs and cultural traditions. In the past symbolism has played an important part in all forms of Chinese art, including that of carpet weaving. To appreciate the designs and motifs fully, it is helpful to understand some of the symbolism.

The Taoist and Buddhist religions each have their own systems of religious symbols. Rugs may include the symbols that represent Taoism's Eight Immortals, virtuous people who had been rewarded with immortality. Likewise, a carpet may depict the *Fo*-dog of Buddhism, defender of law and protector of shrines.

The Chinese language has many homonyms, words that are spelled differently (with different characters) but are pronounced in the same way. The Chinese words for bat and happiness, each a different character in Chinese script, are pronounced the same (*fu*). Consequently, the bat was used in Chinese art as a symbol representing happiness.

For a more detailed discussion of Chinese rugs, see *Affordable Oriental Rugs.**

INDIA

KNOT:	*Persian*
WARP:	*cotton (jute in some older rugs)*
WEFT:	*cotton; single or double*
PILE:	*medium to medium short wool*
FRINGE:	*narrow* kelim *with knotted fringe at both ends*
SELVEDGE:	*overcast with wool*

Hand-knotted carpets have been woven in India since the sixteenth century when the Moghul Emperor, Akbar the Great, founded the Indian carpet weaving industry. He brought Persian weavers from Kashan, Isfahan, and Kerman to his courts and established workshops for the weaving of carpets.

Today, the major weaving centers in India are the Mirzapur-Bhadohi area, Agra, Jaipur, Amritsar, and Srinagar. The Mirzapur-Bhadohi area

---

* Janice Summers Herbert, *Affordable Oriental Rugs* (New York: Macmillan, 1980).

PLATE 104: *INDO-TABRIZ (Hunting Design)*
3 ft. by 5 ft. Courtesy of Mr. and Mrs. Hayes Jenkins

alone accounts for almost 90 percent of India's total carpet production. Rugs are also woven in other areas scattered throughout the country, but their total output is relatively small.

The majority of Indian carpets are custom made with specified designs, colors, sizes, and quality ranges. The ability of Indian weavers to adapt designs to meet market demands, and to vary the tightness and type of weave, has given Indian rugs and carpets a competitive edge of the world's markets.

Rug importers will order and stock rugs with the same design in varying grades. Each importer will identify and label each quality grade with his own trademarked name. It is impossible to rely upon these names or trademarks to differentiate between the quality of rugs from different importers. When comparing rugs from different importers, an evaluation must be made on a direct analysis of the rugs.

Indian carpets are woven with a Persian knot on a cotton foundation. The wool used for the pile is generally good quality. However, the quality of wool and the coarseness of the weave can vary greatly, depending on the quality of carpet.

The Indian weavers adopt and adapt numerous Persian, Turkish, Caucasian, Turkoman, French Savonnerie, and Chinese carpet designs. To denote their Indian origin, these patterns are often prefixed with "Indo," for example, Indo-Savonnerie, or Indo-Tabriz. The designs and motifs of the Indo-Savonnerie and Indo-Chinese carpets are quite often accentuated by a "carving" of the pile. The carved pile imparts a three-dimensional effect, further accentuating the motifs.

PLATE 105: *INDO-CHINESE DESIGN*
3 ft. 1 in. by 5 ft. 1 in.
Courtesy of Dr. and
Mrs. Wilbur Veith

PAKISTAN

KNOT: *Persian*
WARP: *cotton (wool in older rugs)*
WEFT: *cotton (wool in older rugs)*
PILE: *short to medium short, silky wool in length*
FRINGE: kelim *with knotted fringe at both ends*
SELVEDGE: *overcast with wool*

Pakistan shares India's four-hundred-year history of carpet weaving. After Pakistan was partitioned from India in 1947, many Moslem weavers left India to settle in Lahore and other parts of Pakistan. Recognizing the need for such industry and employment, the new Pakistani government granted subsidies to the carpet industry. This financial support allowed Pakistani rugs to be priced very attractively on foreign markets.

Pakistani carpets are finely woven; a Persian knot is used on a cotton foundation. In most Pakistani rugs, the wool used for the pile is of good quality from local sheep. The best quality rugs use local wool blended with wool imported from Australia; Australian wool contains more lanolin and is stronger, yielding a more durable and lustrous carpet. Pakistani rugs are noted for their rich sheen, due largely to the chemical (or "luster") wash given the carpets before they are exported.

Pakistani designs are crisp and well-defined, and have been adopted or adapted from those of other weaving centers. The Bukhara, one of the most

PLATE 106: *GHIORDES PRAYER DESIGN 2 ft. 5 in. by 4 ft. 1 in.*

PLATE 107: *PAKISTAN BUKHARA, 3 ft. 1 in. by 5 ft. 2 in.*

popular and widely known of the Pakistani designs, was adopted from the tribal designs of the Turkomans. This design is one of small repeated rectilinear motifs, each of which is called a *gul*.

A wide variety of designs that originated with Persian rugs are woven in Pakistan. They include medallion designs that resemble those of Tabriz and Kashan; prayer designs of Kashan; and the all-over Shah Abbas design of Tabriz, Kashan, and Isfahan.

The most common Turkish designs adopted by the Pakistanis are the Ghiordes prayer and *saff* designs. The Ghiordes prayer was one of the first designs woven in Pakistani rugs; on either side of the field, columns extend upward to support the *mihrab* or prayer arch. The *saff* design is that of multiple *mihrabs*, ranging in number from two to nine.

The brilliant colors and bold geometric designs of the Caucasian rugs are also used in Pakistani rugs. Designs traditionally associated with Kazak, Shirvan, and Kuba are the most frequently copied.

Hand-knotted carpets are woven throughout Pakistan. The greatest concentration of weaving is located around the cities of Lahore, Karachi, and Peshawar. Lahore and the surrounding Punjab province account for 85 percent of the country's total production. Reasonable prices, crisp designs, and silky appearance have made Pakistani carpets quite popular.

For a more detailed treatment of the rugs from India and Pakistan, see *Affordable Oriental Rugs.*

Kelims and Pileless Carpets

PILELESS CARPETS are the oldest and most widespread form of handmade carpets. Although their precise origins have been lost in antiquity, they have been woven for several thousand years. Hand-woven on looms, these carpets are known throughout the world by many different names, depending on their structural characteristics and use. One may hear them referred to by such names as kelims, dhurries, palas, scoarta, soumaks, and flatweaves.

Throughout Iran, Turkey, the Caucasus, Turkestan, India, and other parts of central Asia, pileless carpets have been woven as inexpensive floor coverings, blankets, saddlebags, and animal trappings.

A kelim or pileless carpet is essentially a weft-faced fabric; weft threads are woven back and forth, across and under the warp threads, completely covering them. Designs in pileless carpets are formed from these colored weft threads.

There are two different weaving techniques found in kelims. These relate to the manner in which two different colors of weft threads meet. The threads may be kept separate, so that each thread doubles back on itself, creating a slit at the juncture; this is referred to as a *slit weave*. The other variation is to have the two different colors of weft threads share a common warp thread, around which both loop in doubling back; this is a *shared warp* weave. (See Figure 23.)

FIGURE 23: *TYPES OF PILELESS WEAVING*

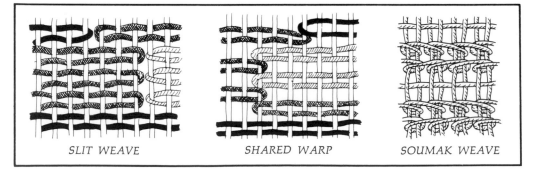

SLIT WEAVE   SHARED WARP   SOUMAK WEAVE

PLATE 108: *SENNA KELIM 4 ft. by 6 ft. Courtesy of Dr. and Mrs. L.A. Graham*

Soumaks are another type of pileless rug; they are woven in the Caucasus and in parts of Turkey and Iran. They possess two types of weft threads. The colored design weft thread is passed over four warp threads and back under two, similar to a chain stitch. The rows of colored wefts alternate, each going in a different direction, to give a herringbone effect (see Figure 23). The other weft thread is used to strengthen the carpet and support the design wefts. When the color weft is changed, the thread is pulled through to the back of the carpet and left to hang. Because its back is an unsightly mass of loose threads, only one side of the soumak is usable.

Senna kelims woven in western Iran by Kurdistan weavers are considered to be among the finest examples of pileless weaving. They are woven with a Herati design almost identical to the knotted-pile Senna rug (see Plate 110).

The Balouchi tribes are known for their numerous pileless weavings. Quite often these kelims have designs that have been brocaded or embroidered. This is done with the addition of an extra weft thread, which is used for the embroidering of the design or motif onto the body of the carpet.

Pileless carpets are woven throughout Turkey in a wide variety of designs and weaving techniques. Quite often, designs and motifs are outlined with an extra strand of yarn, which is wrapped around the warp threads. This serves several purposes: first, it covers the slits which are formed by the juncture of the two colored weft threads; second, it accentuates the designs and motifs.

In the Caucasus, kelims were referred to as *palas*. The majority of

PLATE 110: *SHIRVAN PALAS* *3 ft. by 5 ft. Courtesy of Hower House*

Caucasian kelims were woven in the Kuba and Shirvan areas, even though they were woven throughout the Caucasus.

There is another type of pileless carpet woven in the Caucasus and parts of Turkey, referred to as *verneh*. These carpets were woven in a kelim or soumak weave with the designs and motifs embroidered or brocaded onto the body of the carpet.

A *dhurrie* is a type of pileless carpet woven in India, Afghanistan, and parts of Pakistan. Originally, dhurries were woven entirely of cotton—both cotton warp and cotton weft threads. Since World War II, however, wool weft threads also have been used. The majority of dhurries now woven have cotton warp threads and wool weft threads.

PLATE 112: *ARDEBIL SOUMAK 4 ft. by 6 ft. Courtesy of Dr. and Mrs. Wilbur Veith*

10 Buying and Caring for an Oriental Rug

THERE ARE no hard-and-fast rules that govern the buying of an Oriental rug. The qualities that made each Oriental rug unique can also prove bewildering when one is confronted with a series of strange names, huge assortments of color combinations, and ranges of quality. Each rug must be evaluated on its own merits, considering its condition, size, design, price, and country of origin.

Prepurchase Considerations

An Oriental rug should be purchased as a work of art. Unfortunately, there are no absolutes that govern the purchase of an Oriental rug. There are, however, some basic guidelines that one should follow and questions that should be kept in mind.

What is the purpose of buying the Oriental rug? Is it utilitarian, for a decorative accent, a capital-gains investment, or a combination of several of these? If the purpose of the rug is strictly utilitarian, will the rug be in a heavy traffic pattern and how well can it be expected to withstand wear?

What is the area to be covered? Establish a minimum and maximum dimension suitable for the intended use of the rug. Rugs are usually paid for (whether quoted in this manner or not) on the basis of total number of square feet, or square meters. It is not economical to buy more rug than one needs.

What is the price range? The buyer should keep in mind the upper limit that he is willing to spend. Don't be pressured to buy a more expensive rug than the intended use warrants.

Where to Buy

There are several sources from which to buy an Oriental rug. The most common are Oriental rug dealers, auctions, individuals, and foreign bazaars.

ORIENTAL RUG DEALERS

Established and reputable Oriental-rug dealers *can be* the single best and most reliable source. They should be able to advise you on the wearing qualities, investment potential, and care of your Oriental rug. The final appraisal and decision, however, lies with the purchaser.

Some dealers may tend to specialize in or overrepresent the rugs of a particular country, a particular range of sizes (carrying mostly room-size rugs, for example), or a narrow price range (either at the low end for volume of sales or the high end for investors or collectors). However, most dealers do carry a wide selection of rugs in a variety of sizes and price ranges. It is advisable to visit all the rug shops in your area to gain a better view of what is available across the broad range of rugs you will encounter.

Choosing a dealer is normally a problem for the first-time rug buyer. It may come down to buying from the dealer who has a rug you want. The careful buyer considers the reputation of the dealer. Word-of-mouth advertising and the recommendation of satisfied customers (especially those who have made several rug purchases) should be given weight.

BUYING AT AUCTION

Many people are lured by the excitement of buying at auction. The hope of obtaining an Oriental rug for a fraction of its worth brings thousands of prospective buyers to auctions each year. The knowledgeable buyer may be able to make some good acquisitions, making careful selections from the wide range of rugs offered.

Buying an Oriental rug at *any* auction entails risks; the type and degree of risk varies with the kind of auction and with the knowledge of the buyer. The successful buyer not only has knowledge of rugs but also is familiar with the procedures and requirements of the auction. No rug purchased at an auction is returnable; the buyer rarely has any recourse if the rug is not as represented, is in need of repair, or if the buyer decides that he does not like it. It is difficult to properly inspect the condition of a rug, and rugs are sold on an "as is" basis.

There are three types of auctions: traveling or itinerant auctions, estate auctions, and those held at established auction houses. Each has its own attributes and benefits, as well as disadvantages.

Traveling Auctions

Traveling auctions go from city to city, selling Oriental rugs in motels or other rented facilities. The auctioneers are master showmen and may have shills (their hired people in the audience) to bid the price up until an acceptable level has been reached. The rug will not be sold for less than a predetermined price that recovers all costs and yields a profit. Such costs include rent of the facility, auctioneer's commission, transportation costs, plus his cost of each rug.

A common misconception of the auction is that all rugs must be sold regardless of price. In the traveling auction, the auctioneer is under no such pressure; if bids do not exceed the auctioneer's minimum, that rug is withdrawn from consideration, to be offered again in the next city on the circuit. Because of all these considerations, the risk is placed on the potential buyer, not on the auctioneer. Only on rare occasions is one able to purchase a rug for an amount less than its worth.

Many of the rugs sold at traveling auctions are rugs that for one reason or another don't sell on the wholesale market, or are wholesaler's rejects. Importers buy in lots, rather than buying individual rugs, so occasionally pieces are encountered that do not meet the wholesale standard of quality. Many of these rugs find their way to the auction block. Not all rugs at auctions are "inferior"; a few good rugs are often deliberately interspersed among the others.

Estate Auctions

In an estate auction the entire furnishings of a specific household are liquidated. Unlike the traveling auctioneer, the estate auctioneer has been commissioned to dispose completely of all items, getting the most revenue possible. As a result, the potential buyer has a good chance of obtaining a rug for less than its value.

Yet risks are also present. At some estate sales, Oriental rugs are brought in to entice greater attendance. These rugs usually come from the stock of Oriental rug or antique dealers and are being sold at a preestablished minimum. In the traveling auction, the bidding is against the house; in the estate auction, one bids against other potential buyers, driving the price up. Rug dealers and other knowledgeable people are more apt to attend estate auctions, so competition can be fierce.

Auction Houses

Established auction houses have their reputations to maintain, as well as higher levels of costs to recoup. The potential buyer here bids against other bidders, but also against the house. The present owner of the rug to be sold has established the opening level for bids. Greater publicity usually attends the auctions of these houses, and collectors as well as dealers may come from afar.

Specialized collections and superior pieces are more likely to be offered by established auction houses because of their expertise, reputation, and ability to obtain the best possible prices for the owners. The prices obtained at these auctions will tend to reflect the actual worth of the rugs, and bargains should not be expected.

Knowledge is a prerequisite at any auction—ability to evaluate rug condition and knowledge of current prices and auction procedures are a must. Not only must the buyer be able to establish a realistic appraisal of what the rug may be worth on the market, he must also be able to set and observe a limit of what the rug is worth to him.

PURCHASING OVERSEAS

Knowledge and understanding of the area's or country's rugs is a necessity when one purchases an Oriental rug abroad. When away from home, buyers are at the mercy of the rug seller. There is little or no recourse if the rug is misrepresented.

Far too often, tourists who think they are getting "the buy of a life-time" could have purchased the same rug at home for much less. The "silk" rug they purchased turns out to be a wool rug that has been given a luster wash, or the "antique" rug has been given a wash to make it appear old. In many cases the rug you purchased may not be the rug that is shipped to your home; a rug of much lesser quality may be substituted.

If you want to purchase an Oriental rug overseas, the best way is to do some comparison shopping at home before you leave. Check the prices of rugs from the countries that you will visit. You will have something with which to compare while abroad. Remember that there are a wide range of qualities and prices available from every country.

Keep in mind that the prices at your local Oriental rug retailer already include the freight charges, customs duty, and any applicable taxes. You will be liable for all of these in addition to your purchase price. In some instances, taxes and freight charges may amount to as much as, or even more than, the purchase price of the rug.

Trade agreements and duty charges vary from country to country, and are subject to change. Check with the proper governmental authorities about the duty or taxes imposed on Oriental rugs. Also verify the required documentation on rugs purchased as antique, and whether there are restrictions on rugs (antique) leaving a country.

Bargains can be found if you are willing to persevere and look for them. Before purchasing, check the prices in several shops; prices can vary greatly within the same bazaar. Bargaining should be done. Don't be pressured into paying more. If possible, take your purchase with you. Rugs can be baled into unbelievably small packages. Your rug might have a few wrinkles when you first get home, but these will eventually come out.

Some countries have government-operated handicraft stores. The prices here may be slightly higher than in a local bazaar, but you can generally be assured that the merchandise is as it is represented.

In China, Romania, and the Soviet Union, rugs may be purchased in stores operated for foreign visitors. The prices are fixed and there is no bargaining, but the merchandise is reasonably priced. Purchases in these stores usually cannot be made in local currency. Although some foreign currency may be disallowed, United States dollars, German deutschmarks, and Swiss francs usually are well received.

Comparing the Rug Sources

The following criteria should help the prospective purchaser evaluate the rug-source alternatives.

Is the price fair? Comparison shop! Rug prices can and do vary from dealer to dealer: rugs of the same type (Chinese rugs of the same 90-line quality, for example), same age, and same size. Since sizes do vary, it is helpful to compute the cost per square foot or per square meter of each rug.

Can the rug be examined thoroughly? Often at auctions or house sales, hasty decisions are forced upon a prospective buyer before a careful inspection of a rug can be made. Objectionable flaws or damage, such as stains, moth damage, holes, slits in the foundation, or crooked edges may go unnoticed at a brief, first glance.

Can the rug be returned? A rug should be taken home on approval to see if it creates the desired effect. This is a standard practice among most reputable Oriental-rug dealers. Ask if the rug can be exchanged or returned for a full credit if the rug does not have the look desired when placed in your home or office.

Does the seller guarantee the rug? There are traveling auctions that may only be in town for several days. The buyer has no recourse if the rug purchased is misrepresented or has serious or objectionable flaws. At house sales, for example, the rug is sold "as is," and the seller assumes no responsibility.

Never be in such a hurry to buy an Oriental rug that you cannot carefully inspect the rug and evaluate its merits. A few extra minutes may save a lot of time, aggravation, and money, if it is later found that costly repairs need to be made.

Bargaining

An Oriental rug may be purchased by making an offer lower than the stipulated or asking price, in much the same way as buying a house or a car. Bargaining is a compromise situation; in bargaining, knowledge is power. The final negotiated price can be strongly influenced by the knowledge of the buyer or seller.

Bargaining situations may be encountered almost anytime a person is trying to buy an Oriental rug, whether from an individual or a rug merchant. A rug dealer has certain costs that have been incurred and his prices tend to reflect current market conditions; therefore, his ability and willingness to bargain are somewhat restricted. An individual's price may have been set rather arbitrarily because of lack of market information and his minimal investment in the rug (the rug may have been inherited or held for some time).

Knowledge in any situation makes the position of the buyer more certain and strategically sound. The more knowledgeable the buyer, the more likely the compromise will be in his favor.

PLATE 113: *The back of a hand-knotted (Tabriz) rug.*

PLATE 114: *The back of a machine-made Oriental design rug.*

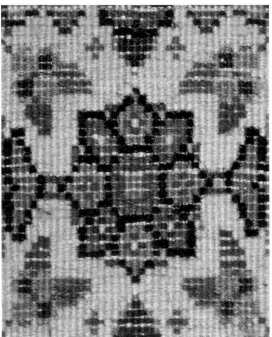

Oriental-Design Rugs

Rugs of Oriental design are widely available under numerous brand names. They have designs that have been copied from Persian, Chinese, and Turkoman carpets.

Oriental-design rugs are machine-made and must not be confused with genuine Oriental rugs. An Oriental rug *must* be hand-made, either hand-knotted or hand-woven. An Oriental-*design* rug, since it is not an Oriental rug, will not maintain its value. Yet Oriental-design rugs often cost as much as, and sometimes more than, a genuine Oriental rug.

Four elements of carpet construction serve as checkpoints in determining whether a rug is a genuine Oriental or a machine-made imitation. These are the back, knots, fringed ends, and sides.

On the back of the machine-made carpet, the design is vague or indistinct; the hand-knotted rug has a design that is as well defined on the back as on the front (see Plates 113 and 114). At times inspecting the back of the carpet is difficult because of a backing such as jute. This is a sure sign that the rug is *not* a genuine Oriental rug.

Fold the carpet and spread the pile; loops of yarn can be seen surrounding the warp threads in a genuine Oriental rug. The pile of a machine-made rug has been attached by either being stitched or glued (see Plates 115 and 116).

The fringe and selvedge offer other points for comparison. The fringe of a genuine Oriental rug is an extension of the carpet's warp threads; the manner in which the fringes are finished vary from one weaving center to another. The fringe of the machine-made rug has been overcast or sewn onto the carpet, and is not a part of the carpet's foundation. See Plates 117, and 118.

The sides, or selvedges, of the machine-made rugs are bound by

PLATE 115: *The pile has been spread to show that each strand of wool has been tied to a pair of warp threads (Alternating warp threads are depressed.) Tabriz carpet with Ghiordes knot.*

PLATE 116: *The pile of this machine-made carpet has been spread to show that the pile is attached without knots.*

PLATE 117: *The knotted fringe of a Tabriz rug.*

PLATE 118: *The overcast fringe of a machine-made Oriental-design rug. Fringe of this type will never be seen on a hand-knotted rug.*

PLATE 119: *The selvedge (hand overcast) on the side of a hand-knotted (Joshaghan) rug.*

PLATE 120: *The machine-stitched overcasting on the side of a machine-made Oriental-design rug. Note the running stitch that secures the selvedge to the body of the carpet.*

machine, or serged, unlike the selvedges on the genuine Oriental rug (see Plates 119 and 120), which are hand-overcast in either cotton or wool.

It is necessary that all four elements of construction be checked before a final evaluation is made. Used Oriental rugs are occasionally found with sides that have been machine-serged or their ends refringed.

Evaluating Condition and Determining Value

The carpet as a whole must be considered before making a detailed investigation of its component parts. If the colors are pleasing and the pattern well executed, then the potential buyer should check the carpet's structure.

EXAMINING THE OVERALL CARPET

Does the carpet lie flat on the floor? Wrinkles or ridges in the rug are caused by improper warp tension and will not come out; they wear rapidly as well as appearing unsightly. Creases caused by the rug's being folded and a slight rippling of the selvedge, however, will come out over a period of time.

Are the sides crooked, or are they relatively straight and parallel to each other? Some slight irregularities in the rug's sides are to be expected, but very crooked rugs are objectionable. Minor irregularities can be corrected by having the rug sized or stretched. This process should be done by the rug dealer before the rug is purchased. The rug should be carefully inspected afterward to ensure that the irregularities have been satisfactorily removed.

Each rug should be carefully inspected to make certain that no borders or portions of borders have been removed, especially the borders at the fringed ends of the rug. The rug should have the same border designs on all four sides and should not have been cut or shortened in any way. Turkoman rugs and Turkoman-design rugs from India and Pakistan are the only exception, since they characteristically have dissimilar sides and borders. See Chapter 6.

The types of dyes and colors of the rug should be given careful consideration because of their effect on fading and running. Have the colors faded or will they run together when the rug is washed? Wiping a damp cloth over the top of a rug is a good test to determine if the dyes are colorfast. A rug in which the dyes have already run should be obvious by the blurred design. By comparing the colors on the front and back of the rug, one can tell whether or not the rug has faded. The back of a faded rug will be much darker than the sunlight-faded front. Aniline dyes will have produced all of these undesirable features, and rugs that have been colored with them should be avoided. See Chapter 2, p. 23 for a discussion of aniline dyes.

AGE

Rugs may be classified into three age groups: new, semi-antique, and antique. A new rug is one that has never been used, although it can be several years old.

For practical purposes, many dealers classify rugs as semi-antique if they are from twenty-five to fifty years old, and as antique if they are more than fifty years old. Technically, a rug must be more than a hundred years old to be classified as an antique. Rugs that fall between the new and semi-antique classifications are termed "used." Their actual age and amount of use may vary considerably. The value of a used rug is generally less than its new and semi-antique counterparts, although it reacquires value with age.

Age does affect the value of a rug, but age must be considered together with condition. An antique rug that has been completely worn out is not valuable just because it is old. However, an antique rug in good condition can be priceless.

STRUCTURE

Examining the structure of any rug is important, yet for a *used* rug it is essential. A used rug will have had many opportunities to have been mistreated or improperly cared for. Many of the results of improper treatment are not immediately apparent on casual inspection.

In examining the structure of a rug, there are five major points to be checked. They are:

pile
warp and weft threads
fringe
selvedges
knots

Pile

The pile should be checked for worn areas, holes, and moth damage. Moth damage may appear on the top of the rug, the pile having been eaten down to the foundation; or it may be hidden on the back of the rug. The portion of the knot that is looped around the warp thread may also have been eaten. When this occurs, there is nothing securing the pile to the foundation of the rug. If this is suspected, one may easily remove a tuft of pile by pulling.

If the pile is well worn, the knots themselves are visible. This may occur in spots, rather than uniformly over all the surface of the rug, as when caused by heavy traffic patterns.

In the pile of older rugs, white knots are sometimes visible. These are knots in the warp or weft threads. All rugs have them, but they are more noticeable in older rugs with low pile. If these are objectionable, they can easily be touched up with any colorfast dye.

Chinese and Chinese-design rugs woven in India often have pile that has been carved or sculptured around the designs and motifs. This should not be confused with moth damage.

If dead or skin wool (see Chapter 2, p. 19) has been used for the pile, the fibers will be brittle and not wear well. In a used rug, worn spots caused by the dead wool will be quite obvious. In a new rug, dead wool can be felt by running one's hand across the pile; the dead wool has a definite coarse, bristly feel. Rugs are rarely woven entirely of dead wool.

Warp and Weft Threads

The warp and the weft threads should be checked for cuts and breaks. The rug should be turned completely over to facilitate this inspection. The cuts or breaks in the warp and weft threads can become serious if not repaired *before* the rug is purchased.

Fringe

An inspection of the fringe should be made to determine if the fringe is the original, or if a replacement fringe has been added. Folding a rug back at the end of the pile is the best way to check whether the fringe is an unbroken extension of the warp threads. In a refringed rug the warp threads will terminate (either by being cut or turned under) and a fringed band attached. A refringed rug is less valuable than a rug with its original fringe, even if the original fringe is not in particularly good condition.

Selvedges

The selvedges bind the sides (terminal warp threads) of the carpet. They do not wear as quickly as the fringe but do on occasion need to be reovercast. The reovercasting should always be done by hand rather than machine.

Knots

The *jufti,* or false knot, has been used in some Indian rugs. The knot is tied around four warp threads instead of the usual two. See Chapter 2, p. 22, *jufti* knot.

Knot Count

A feature basic to the construction of all Oriental rugs is the tightness of weave, usually referred to as a rug's "knot count." This is simply the number of knots in a given area, and is quoted either in knots per square inch or per square meter. The number of knots per square inch may vary from as few as 10 to as many as 500, while knots per square meter may range from 16,000 to 800,000. Chart 2 converts knots per square inch to knots per square meter and vice versa. Knot count can be an important tool in evaluating the quality of an Oriental rug—but only when it is properly used.

The assumption quite often made is that "the higher the knot count, the better or more desirable the rug." This is generally true, but there are too many factors involved for this statement always to be accurate.

An antique Khotan rug from the Xinjiang province of China will be more valuable than an Indian carpet of the same knot count, age, and condition, simply because Khotan rugs are more scarce. Knot count should be used only when comparing rugs from the same weaving center, in the same condition, and of the same age. Each rug possesses its own attributes and is unique unto itself, further complicating comparisons between rugs.

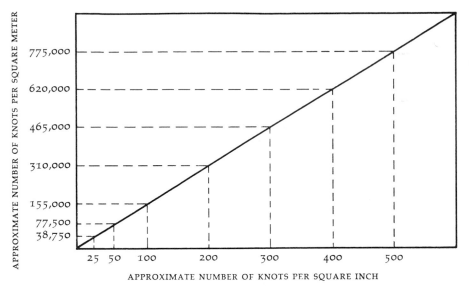

CHART 2: *KNOT-COUNT CONVERSION CHART*

To convert knots per square inch to knots per square meter, find the approximate number of knots per square inch along the horizontal axis of Chart 2. Draw an imaginary line (or follow one of the lines provided) to the heavy diagonal line, then draw an imaginary line from that point of intersection to the vertical axis and read the approximate number of knots per square meter. To convert knots per square meter to knots per square inch, reverse the procedure. For example, a rug with 200 knots per square inch has approximately 310,000 knots per square meter.

Several countries have a different way of denoting the quality of their Oriental rugs. In China, the term *line* (e.g., 90 line) is used; this designation can be converted to the more common number of knots per square inch. The number associated with the term *line* is the number of pairs of warp threads per linear foot; this in turn is the same as the number of knots per linear foot. A 90-line rug has 90 knots per linear foot, both horizontally and vertically, which is equivalent to approximately 54 knots per square inch (90/12 x 90/12 = 54).

Each weaving center has its own characteristic range of knot counts (see Appendix). Individual rugs from the same weaving center, however, do vary in knot count.

Knot count is calculated by counting the number of loops (knot backs) that fall within a 1-inch (or 1-meter) square. Lay a ruler along a weft thread on the back of the rug; count the number of knots in an inch (meter). (When knots are tied on warp threads on the same level, each knot will have two loops clearly visible.) Multiplying the two numbers together gives the number of knots per square inch (meter). This should be done in five different areas scattered over the back of the rug, and those results averaged.

Rugs with higher knot counts have a denser pile than those with lower knot counts. A dense pile gives a sturdier, more durable rug. The pile of high-knot-count rugs is usually cut shorter, yielding a crisp design. These rugs are relatively more expensive than those with lower knot counts.

Each of the points discussed does affect the value of a rug, and the price should reflect the overall condition of the rug. A small flaw that might be objectionable to one person is not always objectionable to another. Since Oriental rugs are individually handcrafted, minor flaws will usually be found; absolute perfection should not be expected. If a rug has a deficiency, it is important that the purchaser be aware of the flaw and how it affects the rug's value; such information is necessary for an informed decision.

Appraisal and Insurance

An Oriental rug should be insured in the same manner and for the same reasons as any other work of art. Most insurance companies require a recent appraisal of the value of the rug by a qualified expert or appraiser in the field. In the case of a recent rug purchase, the bill of sale usually is sufficient to establish its value.

Oriental rug dealers usually provide the service of issuing an insurance appraisal free when a rug is purchased from them. However, a fee is charged for appraising a rug when the rug has been purchased elsewhere.

The basis for the charge and the amount charged for the appraisal can vary greatly. It is advisable to check the fee basis or estimated charge before enlisting the service. Ideally and most fairly, an appraisal fee should be based on the amount of time required to do the appraising or on a charge-per-rug basis.

Most appraisers compute their fee as a percentage of the rug value, typically ranging from one percent (for a large or valuable collection) to five percent (for a single or inexpensive rug); the usual rate is two percent. This can be quite expensive, so be sure to determine the fee basis before agreeing to that appraiser's service. Negotiating a lower fee may prove useful.

The appraisal should be typed on the appraiser's stationery, with his or her address and telephone number. The owner's name and address also should be on the appraisal. Each rug should be separately identified by size, origin, age, and any identifying characteristics; each rug should have a separate dollar value designated. Two copies should be made, one for the appraiser's files, one for the insurance company; the original goes to the owner.

The evaluation should be for the amount of money required to replace each particular rug. Such an appraisal, preferably with a photograph of the rug or rugs, should be maintained by the insurance company in the event (God forbid!) of a claim, such as a theft or damage. Oriental rugs are not depreciated by reputable insurance companies; the appraisal establishes replacement value, on which reimbursement is made. A professional insurance agent can provide information on Oriental rug insurance coverage to best fit the needs and situation of the client.

Care

Oriental rugs require surprisingly little care. Dirt does not penetrate these rugs, as it does machine-made carpeting, although soil will eventually work its way to the base of the pile. Depending on the amount of traffic they undergo, rugs should be cleaned every three to five years. Cleaning should be done by a reputable firm that specializes in the cleaning of Oriental rugs. Proper cleaning is essential; steam-cleaning, dry-cleaning, and certain chemical processes remove the natural oils and cause the pile to become brittle and wear more rapidly.

In the regular vacuuming of Oriental rugs, the vacuum cleaner should move in the same direction as the nap of the carpet. The direction of the nap can be determined by running the hand across the pile (from fringe to fringe). Vacuuming against the grain presses the dirt back into the carpet. The fringe of a carpet should never be vacuumed, but swept with a broom. The continued catching of the fringe in the suction of a vacuum causes it to break and tear. Sweeping the carpet with a broom also helps bring out the natural patina or sheen in the rug.

Oriental rugs have the remarkable ability to withstand wear. Their life span is at least three or four times that of machine-made commercial carpeting. A good-quality pad helps protect the rug and prolongs its life even more. The best padding for an Oriental rug is hair- or fiber-filled with rubberized surfaces to keep the rug from moving or wrinkling.

Spills of virtually any nature may be removed without permanent stain if taken care of in time. Dilute the spill with plenty of water, and blot the wet area until *all* of the moisture is removed. Failure to remove all of the moisture might result in mildew.

Moths can cause extensive damage to Oriental rugs. Not only do moths eat the pile but they also eat the knots on the back of the rug. Moths are especially attracted to dark, relatively undisturbed areas, such as those under furniture. It is quite simple to eliminate these pests and safeguard against their return. Both the front and back of a carpet should be sprayed about every six months with any one of a number of moth sprays available on the market.

If a rug or carpet needs to be stored, it should be mothproofed, rolled (not folded), and put in a dry, moth-free environment.

The leakage of potted plants can inflict costly damage on an Oriental rug. The constant seepage or condensation of water on the bottom of the pot causes the foundation and the pile to rot. Never place a potted plant on an Oriental rug and be very cautious about placing a plant near one.

Repair

Repairs may be necessary during the life of an Oriental rug, but they should be undertaken only by an expert. Common minor repairs include having the fringed ends secured and reinforced, or the selvedges reovercast; these are relatively inexpensive and should be done in order to prevent the loss, knot by knot, of the pile. Even minor repairs, such as worn fringe or selvedge, can rapidly develop into a serious problem.

Repairing holes in the warp and weft threads, or reweaving moth-damaged areas of the pile, can be done but may be quite costly. This should be done only after consideration of how much the rug is worth. An excellent repair should not be detected with a casual glance. If in doubt about the qualifications of a repairer, ask to see examples of his finished repair work.

As with any work or work of art, an Oriental rug must have proper care.

Oriental rugs are not only beautiful, they are also the most practical home furnishing you can buy. They enhance any decor with their beauty, and make a room an individual creation. Given proper care, the Oriental rug will be a durable floor covering as well as a treasured work of art.

APPENDIX I

Summary Chart of Oriental Rugs, by Availability, Durability, Price, Typical Knot Count, and Common Rug Sizes

LEGEND: In the columns headed "Availability," "Durability," and "Price," the numbers express the relative availability, durability, and price of the rugs listed; a "1" indicates a rug that is *not* relatively available or durable, and is of *low* price. A "5" indicates a rug that is relatively widely available, is very durable, and of high price.

	Availability	Durability	Price	50–150	151–250	251–350	251–350	More than 450	2 x 4 or smaller	3 x 5 to 6 x 9	8 x 10 or larger
IRAN											
Abadeh	3	4	4		x				x	x	
Afshar	1	3	3	x					x	x	
Arak/Sultanabad	3	4	3		x						x
Ardebil	5	4	3			x			x	x	x
Balouchi	4	2	2	x					x	x	
Bibikabad	3	2	2	x							x
Bijar	1	4	4		x					x	
Dergazine	5	3	2		x				x	x	x
Ferahan	1	3	4		x					x	
Hamadan	5	3	3	x					x	x	
Herez	4	3	3		x						x
Ingeles	3	4	3	x						x	
Isfahan	3	5	5				x	x		x	
Joshaghan	3	4	4			x				x	
Karaja	4	4	3		x				x	x	
Kashan	4	4	4			x	x		x	x	x
Kerman	5	4	3			x			x	x	x
Kurd	3	4	3	x					x	x	
Lillihan	3	3	2	x					x	x	
Mahal	3	2	2	x							x
Malayer	2	4	4	x						x	x
Mashad	3	3	3		x					x	x
Meshkin	3	3	2	x						x	x
Mud	4	4	4		x					x	x
Nain	3	5	5				x	x	x	x	
Qashqai	2	3	4	x					x	x	
Qum	4	5	5			x				x	
Sarouk	4	4	4		x				x	x	x
Senna	1	4	4			x				x	
Sennabaff	4	4	3			x				x	x
Seraband	4	3	3		x					x	x
Shiraz	4	2	3	x					x	x	x
Tabriz	5	5	5			x			x	x	x
Veramin	1	4	4		x					x	
Yelemeh	4	3	4	x					x	x	
Yezd	1	4	4		x					x	x
CAUCASIAN											
Baku	1	3	5*		x					x	
Daghestan	1	3	5*	x						x	
Derbend	1	3	5*	x							x

Table 1

	AVAILABILITY	DURABILITY	PRICE	50–150	151–250	251–350	351–450	MORE THAN 450	2 x 4 OR SMALLER	3 x 5 TO 6 x 9	8 x 10 OR LARGER
Bergama	1	4	5	x						x	
Döşemealti	2	3	2	x						x	
Ezine	1	3	4	x						x	
Hereke silk	2	3	5				x	x		x	
wool	1	5	4				x			x	
Kayseri artificial silk	4	1	3	x					x	x	
silk	1	3	4					x	x	x	
wool	2	4	3		x					x	
Kirşehir	3	3	3	x						x	
Konya	2	4	3	x						x	
Kozak	1	4	4	x						x	
Kula	3	3	3	x						x	
Ladik	2	3	4		x					x	
Melas	3	4	3	x						x	
Yağcibedir	3	3	3	x						x	
Yahyali	3	3	3	x						x	
CHINA	5	4†	3†	x					x	x	x
PAKISTAN	5	3†	1†	x					x	x	x
INDIA	5	2†	1†	x					x	x	x

Table 2

	AVAILABILITY	DURABILITY	PRICE	50–150	151–250	251–350	351–450	MORE THAN 450	2 x 4 OR SMALLER	3 x 5 TO 6 x 9	8 x 10 OR LARGER
Gendge	1	3	5*	x						x	
Karabagh	1	3	5*	x	x					x	x
Kazak	2	3	5*	x					x	x	
Kuba	2	3	5*	x	x					x	
Shirvan	2	3	5*	x	x					x	
Talish	1	3	5*	x						x	
New Caucasian (USSR)	1	3	4	x	x				x	x	x
TURKOMAN											
Afghan	3	4	3	x					x	x	x
Daulatabad	2	4	4	x						x	
Ersari	1	3	4	x						x	
Khotan	1	2	3	x					x	x	
Mauri	2	4	4		x					x	x
Salor	1	4	4			x			x	x	
Sariq	1	3	4		x				x	x	
Tekke	2	3	4		x				x	x	
Yomud	2	3	4	x					x	x	
New Turkoman											
(Iran)	1	3	4		x				x	x	
(USSR)	1	3	4		x				x	x	
TURKEY											
Ayvacik	1	3	4	x						x	

* Because most of the available Caucasian rugs are semi-antique or antique, very few will be found in excellent condition. All rug prices are strongly influenced by condition; rugs in excellent condition will bring top prices. Prices drop drastically for anything less than good condition.

† Variations in durability and price are extreme, depending on quality. Index numbers should be regarded as an average only.

APPENDIX II

Pronunciation Guide

BELOW ARE SUGGESTED PRONUNCIATIONS for terms used in this book. The terms include the names of places and tribes, as well as technical terms used to describe some aspect of an Oriental rug.

The reader should be aware that the pronunciations have been selected to be those most representative of what he or she will hear in an Oriental rug context. That is, some pronunciations do not quite capture the exact way a native might pronounce the term. In these cases, it is felt that being understood is better than being "right."

Also, one should remember that these terms are derived from non-English alphabets and employ sounds for which the English language has no parallel. As a result, the phonetic transliteration must approximate the native sound, as judged by the translator. One is therefore likely to encounter different spellings and pronunciations for the same term, depending on the source.

Abadeh	AB-ah-deh	Kuba	KOO-bah
Arak	ah-RAK	Kula	KOO-lah
Ardebil	AHR-deh-beel	Kurd	KURD
Ayvacik	ah-vah-jek	Lâdik	lah-DEEK
Baku	bah-KOO	Lillihan	LILL-ih-han
Balouchi	bah-LOOCH-ee	Mahal	mah-HAWL
Bergama	BER-gah-mah	Malayer	mah-LAY-urr
Bibikabad	beh-BIK-ah-bad	Mashad	mah-SHAD
Bijar	BEE-jahr	Mauri	MOHR-ree
Bukhara	booh-KAHR-ah	Meshkin	mesh-KIHN
Daghestan	DAG-eh-stan	Melas	mee-LAHS
Daulatabad	daw-LAT-ah-bad	Mud	MOOD
Dergazine	DER-geh-zeen	Nain	ny-EEN
Döşemealti	DUH-sheh-MELL-TEE	Palas	pah-LAY
Ersari	urr-SAH-ree	Qashqai	KASH-guy
Ezine	eh-ZEEN	Qum	koom or goom
Ferahan	fer-aw-HAWN	Salor	sah-LOHR
Gendge	GEHN-jee	Sariq	sah-REEK
Hamadan	HAM-ah-dan	Sarouk	sah-ROOK
Hereke	heh-REE-kee	Senna	SEHN-nah
Herez	heh-REEZ	Seraband	sehr-ah-BAND
Ingeles	ENN-geh-lahs	Shiraz	sheer-AHS
Isfahan	ESS-fah-hahn	Shirvan	sheer-VAHN
Joshaghan	JAW'sh-gun	Soumak	soo-MAHK
Karaja	kah-RAH-jah	Tabriz	tah-BREEZ
Kashan	kah-SHAWN	Talish	tah-LEESH
Kayseri	KAH-zer-i	Tekke	TEHK-ee
Kazak	kah-ZAK	Xinjiang	zing-j'yang
Kelim	kee-LEEM or gee-LEEM	Yagcibedir	YAYG-jee-beh-DEER
Kerman	KER-man	Yahyali	yah-YAH-lee
Khotan	KO-tan	Yelemeh	YEH-leh-meh
Khurasan	KHOHR-ah-sawn	Yestik	yez-TEEK
Kirşehir	KERR-sheh-HEER	Yezd	YAHZ'D or YEHZ'D
Konya	KOHN-yah	Yomud	yoh-MOOD
Kozak	KO-zakh		

GLOSSARY AND RUG TERMS

ABRASH   a color variation or stripe of a slightly different hue across the body of the carpet. This is the result of a slight color difference in the dye lots used.

ANATOLIAN   a name loosely applied to all Turkish rugs from the Anatolian plateau.

ARA-KHACHI   middle or main border (*see* BALA-KHACHI).

AUBUSSON   a pileless (flatweave) rug, generally with a floral medallion in pastel colors, once woven in France. The designs of these rugs have been adopted and adapted to pile carpets, and are now woven in India and China.

AY GUL   moon-shaped motif used as the medallion in rugs from Eastern Turkestan.

BAFF   the Persian word for knot.

BALA-KHACHI   small border stripe on either side of the main border (*see* ARA-KHACHI).

BERDELIK   wall hanging; silk rugs generally fit into this category.

BID MAJNUM   weeping willow design, or a combination of weeping willow, cyprus, and poplar trees.

BORDER   a band or series of bands surrounding the interior, and major attraction, of the carpet—its ground or field.

BOTEH   a small motif that resembles a pine cone or pear. See Plates 9-14, pg. oo.

BUKHARA   name associated with Turkoman-design rugs woven in India and Pakistan; also, an ancient marketplace for the rugs of Turkestan.

CARTOON   a piece of graphlike paper on which the rug pattern has been drawn. It is used as a guide in weaving the rug, each square represents a single knot, the color of which is keyed to the color of the square (*see* TALIM).

CARTOUCHE   a cloudlike enclosure which surrounds a date or an inscription woven into a rug.

CARVED PILE   grooves cut into the pile to accentuate further the borders and designs. This is done in some Chinese and Indian carpets.

CAUCASIAN   refers to rugs woven in the Caucasus Mountain region of the Soviet Union. The patterns of these rugs are brightly colored and highly stylized.

CEYREK   Turkish term for small rugs, measuring approximately 90 by 140 cm (2 feet 9 inches by 4 feet 6 inches).

CHUVAL   large storage bag usually hung from the interior framework of the Turkoman *yurt* (tent).

CLOSED BACK   a term referring to the appearance of the back of a Chinese carpet. The weft threads of a closed-back carpet are not visible when the carpet is observed from the back; the knots completely cover them.

DASGAH   loom.

DHURRIE   a pileless carpet, usually woven in India with either cotton or wool. The design is created by interweaving colored weft threads through the warp threads.

DOZAR   refers to carpets 4 by 6 feet in size.

EMBOSSED   sculptured pile, or pile that has been woven longer than the rest of the ground and then trimmed to give a relief effect.

ENGSI   piled rug used to cover the doorway of a Turkoman tent.

FOUNDATION   collective term referring to both the warp and weft threads of a carpet.

FRINGE   the loose ends of a carpet's warp threads emerging from the upper and lower ends of the carpet; it may be either knotted or plain.

GHIORDES KNOT   Turkish knot; the knot encircles both warp threads.

GUL   Turkoman tribal emblem, once unique to the Turkoman tribe that wove them. Different Turkoman tribal *guls* have since been adopted by the weaving centers of India and Pakistan.

GULI HENNA   pattern with small yellow plant shape set in rows with profuse flower forms uniting them in a diamond arrangement.

HALI   Turkish word for carpet.

HARSHANG   crab design; pattern with large motifs similar to the Shah Abbas pattern which suggest a crab.

HATCHLOU   originally a Turkoman design, in which the field is divided into quadrants by wide bars or stripes.

HERATI   pattern that consists of a rosette surrounded by four leaves or "fish." The rosette is usually found inside a diamond shape (lozenge), although it need not be.

IPEKLI   artificial silk carpets; the pile is a blend of mercerized cotton and silk waste or rayon.

JUFTI KNOT "false knot"; a modified Turkish or Persian knot, in which the weaver uses four warp threads per knot instead of two.

KELEYGHI Persian term for a rug measuring approximately 6 by 12 feet (2 by 4 meters).

KELIM a pileless rug created by interweaving colored weft threads through the warp threads; or, a finished terminal portion of a carpet falling between the pile and the fringe.

KELLEI Persian term for a large rectangular carpet, measuring approximately 7½ by 18 feet (2½ by 6 meters). (Also called Ghali.)

KENAREH Persian term for runners measuring approximately 3 by 18 feet (2 by 6 meters).

KIABA refers to a rug approximately 6 by 9 feet (2 by 3 meters) in size.

KIS (KIZ) Turkish for "girl" or "bride." When used in conjunction with a type of rug, the term indicates a rug given as a wedding gift from bride to groom.

LECHAI corner design in a rug.

LECHEK TORUNJ any design with corner and central medallions.

LINE a term referring to the number of pairs of warp threads, or knots per linear foot.

MAFRASH large saddlebag.

MIHRAB arch or niche of a prayer rug.

MINA KHANI design comprised of repeated floral motifs surrounded by four similar smaller flowers joined by vines to form a diamond arrangement.

MORGI "hen" pattern, an imaginative design resembling a chicken, which was originated by the Afshari tribe.

MUSKA small triangular shapes, symbols of good luck, which are often woven into Turkish rugs.

NAGZH Persian word for the pattern.

OPEN BACK a term referring to the appearance of the back of a Chinese carpet. The weft threads of an open-back carpet are clearly visible when observing the back of the carpet.

PALAS a Caucasian *kelim*.

PANEL DESIGN design in which the field is divided into rectangular compartments, each of which encloses one or more motifs.

PATINA the sheen acquired by the pile of the rug with age and use.

PERSIAN KNOT Senna knot; a strand of wool encircles one warp thread and winds loosely around the other.

PILE nap of the rug; the clipped ends of the knotted wool.

PUSHTI Persian term for a small pillow cover, approximately 2 by 3 feet (60 by 90 cm).

SAFF "family" prayer rug that has multiple *mihrabs* in a series.

SAVONNERIE a rug hand-knotted in France, with a thick, heavy pile and pastel colors. New copies are now being woven in India.

SCULPTURED PILE embossed pile, or pile that has been woven longer than the rest of the ground and then trimmed to give a relief effect.

SECCADES Turkish term for carpets that measure approximately 120 by 200 cm (3 feet 9 inches by 6 feet 6 inches).

SEDJADEH Persian term for a carpet measuring approximately 7 by 10 feet.

SELVEDGE the sides of a carpet, which have been overcast with wool or cotton for reinforcement.

SENNA KNOT Persian knot; encircles one warp thread and winds loosely around the other.

SHAH ABBAS patron of carpet-making (A.D. 1571–1629); also the pattern with an all-over design with various types of palmettes, cloudbands, and vases interconnected by some form of stalk or tendril.

SHOU Chinese character that symbolizes long life.

SKIRT an additional panel or band woven at the top and bottom of most Turkoman-design rugs.

SPANDREL the portion of the prayer rug which appears above and on either side of the mihrab. See Plate 20.

SWASTIKA Chinese symbol for luck.

TALIM a piece of paper on which the design of a carpet has been written out, knot by knot. (Cf. *cartoon.*)

TAMGAS tribal emblem occasionally woven into Turkish carpets.

TCHUVAL *See* CHUVAL.

TORBA storage bag.

TURBEHLIK   grave carpet, spread over graves as those in the West spread flowers. This rug is the combined handiwork of every member of the household as an expression of sorrow.

TURKISH KNOT   Ghiordes knot; a strand of wool that encircles two warp threads, with the loose ends drawn tightly between the two.

TURKOMAN   refers to rugs from the Turkestan region; their patterns are made up of repeated *guls* (geometric motifs) that were once unique to each tribe.

WARP   threads running longitudinally through the fabric (anchored to the loom).

WEFT   threads running perpendicular to the warp (left to right); these are used to secure the knots in place.

YESTIK   Turkish term for small rugs or mats measuring approximately 50 by 100 cm (1 foot 6 inches by 3 feet 3 inches).

YÜRÜK   name loosely applied to the numerous nomadic tribes residing throughout the Anatolian plateau.

ZARONIM   Persian term for rugs measuring approximately 107 by 150 cm (3 feet 5 inches by 5 feet).

ZARQUART   Persian term for rugs measuring approximately 2 feet by 4 feet.

ZIL-I-SOLTAN   "vase of roses" design; multiple rows of repeated vases of roses.

FOR FURTHER READING

GENERAL

Bennett, Ian. ed. *Rugs and Carpets of the World* (New York: A & W Publishers, Inc., 1977).

Denny, Walter. *Oriental Rugs* (Washington, D.C.: Smithsonian Institution, 1979).

Eiland, Murray. *Orientals Rugs* (Boston: New York Graphic Society, 1976).

Erdmann, Kurt. *Oriental Carpets* (Basingstoke, England: The Crosby Press, 1976).

Fokker, Nicolas. *Oriental Carpets for Today* (Garden City, New York: Doubleday and Co., 1973).

Herbert, Janice S. *Affordable Oriental Rugs* (New York: Macmillan Publishing Co., Inc., 1980).

Hubel, Reinhard. *The Book of Carpets* (New York: Praeger Publishers, 1970).

Izmidlian, Georges. *Oriental Rugs and Carpets Today* (New York: Hippocrene Books, Inc., 1977).

Jerrehian, Aran. *Oriental Rug Primer* (New York: Facts on File, 1980).

Larson, Knut. *Rugs and Carpets of the Orient* (London: Frederick Warne and Co., Ltd., 1966).

Neff, I. and C. Maggs. *Dictionary of Oriental Rugs* (London: Ad. Donker, Ltd., 1977).

PERSIAN

Edwards, A. Cecil. *The Persian Carpet* (London: Duckworth, 1953).

Gans-Reudin, E. *The Splendor of Persian Carpets* (New York: Rizzoli, 1978).

TURKOMAN

Azadi, Siawosch. *Turkoman Carpets* (Basingstoke, England: The Crosby Press, 1975).

Bidder, Hans. *Carpets from Eastern Turkestan* (Accokeek, Maryland: Washington International Associates, 1979).

Mackie, L. and Jon Thompson. *Turkmen* (Washington, D.C.: The Textile Museum, 1980).

O'Bannon, George W. *The Turkoman Carpet.* (London: Duckworth, 1974).

BALOUCHI

Black, D. and C. Loveless. *Rugs of the Wandering Balouchi* (London: David Black Oriental Carpets, 1976).

Konieczny, M. G. *Textiles of Balouchistan* (London: British Museum Publications Ltd., 1979).

CAUCASIAN

Schurmann, Ulrich. *Caucasian Rugs.* (Basingstoke, England: The Crosby Press, 1964).
Wright, Richard. *Rugs and Flat Weaves of the Transcaucasus* (Pittsburgh: Pittsburgh Rug Society, 1980).

TURKEY

Iten-Maritz, J. *Turkish Carpets* (Tokyo: Kodansha International, 1975).

PILELESS CARPETS

Justin, Valerie S. *Flat Woven Rugs of the World* (New York: Van Nostrand Reinhold Co., 1980).
Petsopoulos, Yanni. *Kilims* (New York: Rizzoli, 1979).

INDIA, PAKISTAN, AND CHINA

Herbert, Janice S. *Affordable Oriental Rugs* (New York: Macmillan Publishing Co., Inc., 1980).

CARE AND REPAIR

Stone, Peter F. *Oriental Rug Repair* (Chicago: Greenleaf Co., 1981).

PERIODICALS

Hali: The International Journal of Oriental Carpets and Textiles, published quarterly, managing editors Michael Franses and Robert Pinner (193a Shirland Road, London W9 2EU, England).
Rug News, published monthly, editor L. Stroh. Subscriptions to Museum Books, Inc., 6 West 37th St., New York, N.Y. 10018.

INDEX

Bold face numbers refer to illustration pages.